The Rag-Picker's Guide to Poetry

The Rag-Picker's Guide to Poetry

POEMS, POETS, PROCESS

Eleanor Wilner and Maurice Manning

EDITORS

The University of Michigan Press
Ann Arbor

Copyright © by the University of Michigan 2013

Published in the United States of America by
The University of Michigan Press
Manufactured in the United States of America
⊗ Printed on acid-free paper

2016 2015 2014   4 3 2

A CIP catalog record for this book is available from the British Library.

Library of Congress Cataloging-in-Publication Data

    The rag-picker's guide to poetry : poems, poets, process / Eleanor Wilner and Maurice Manning, editors.
       pages cm
    ISBN 978-0-472-07203-3 (cloth : alk. pbk.) — ISBN 978-0-472-05203-5 (pbk. : alk. pbk.) — ISBN 978-0-472-02967-9 (e-book)
      1. Poetry—Authorship. 2. Poetics. 3. Poetry, American—21st century. I. Wilner, Eleanor, editor of compilation. II. Manning, Maurice, 1966– editor of compilation.
    PN1059.A9R34   2013
    808.1—dc23   2013025445

Contents

Eleanor Wilner and Maurice Manning

Introduction

That we see poets as "rag-pickers" points to our place in time, to the way we con-temporary poets forage wherever something of value and use might be found as material or form—in the past, in the woods, in the world's literature and art, in pop culture, in public events, in chance encounters, in the landfills of history, in "the rag and bone shop of the heart"—a constant, inventive recycling of what can be used to create what we need. "The poem engages in a sort of network-er's pleasure," says Heather McHugh, "making its cat's cradle using the oddest threads it could find, in the spool-rooms of yammer and yarn."

What we can discover in a poem, its shapely or dissonant suggestion—in Robert Frost's words, "the figure a poem makes"—is found only in the process of writing it, as we begin to discern the shadowy shape that moves under the various figures and in the music of the lines, and so help it to fuller emergence. The poem, if it is to be a poem at all, must find its way as it goes and can't be consciously constructed or planned in advance. But how, in Ellen Bryant Voigt's words, to "avoid what's unchallenged and self-protective" and to find, as David Baker says, "not what I thought I would say, but what, in the process of discovery and linkage, error and spillage, I have to say."

The venture of this collection is to look, from the many vantages that the poets in this eclectic anthology chose to look, at what it was—knowing that a poem can't be conceived in advance of its creation—that nevertheless helped their poems to emerge or connected them over time. And to see how the me-ticulous and the spontaneous come together in this process. If preexisting "sub-jects" or preordained endings are deadly, what kind of materials, decisions, or intentions invite the imagination? What triggers what Linda Gregerson calls "that blessed ambush they used to call the Muse," that self-renewing source that refreshes and enlarges vision?

The unexpected sources of poetic provocation are as motley and unclassifiable as the poets in this collection: for Marianne Boruch, time spent in the dissection lab eventuated in a series of poems spoken by a very lively cadaver; for Tony Hoagland, Oscar Wilde and theatrical repartee led him to poems where the amusing talk of characters replaced the narrative of self; for A. Van Jordan, silent films offered cinematic cues and fresh angles of vision for poetry.

The nuclear arms race, the practice of meditation, and Bach's St. Matthew Passion came together for Alan Williamson in a public poem imagined as a collective recitation while dismantling a hydrogen bomb. Michael Collier writes of how the upheavals of the first decade of the twenty-first century induced him to respond, to press back, as Wallace Stevens said the imagination must, against the violent pressure of reality.

"I write, or scrawl, rough, sprawling first drafts from scraps—images, sounds," writes Joan Aleshire. Then the work begins. But first, those essential scraps: "images, sounds"—an inexhaustible supply of metaphoric vision and idiosyncratic music opens from those two endlessly expansive words. For Rick Barot, it was Lucky's sudden torrent of nonsensical speech in *Waiting for Godot* that awakened new energies in him; for Thomas Lux it was a striking image, "a pier as a disappointed bridge," that became an ars poetica; and for Daniel Tobin, a long reach of thought found its complex structure in lines resembling a jetty's extension from the shore.

For Roger Fanning, a Norwegian folk tale, a happy night, and the suicidal dangers of ambiguity emotionally fueled the poems in this anthology; for Karen Brennan, it was the city that opened a "real enough world," while for Jennifer Grotz, the inner world flowered through close observation of landscape; for Mary Leader, the visual language of stitchery—embroidery, the sampler, quilts—created her experimental, rebellious poetic form.

Sometimes it was homage to earlier masters that led poets on: for Reginald Gibbons, it was the Russian poet Boris Pasternak's way of moving, "veering to the next image or idea because the sounds of words draw it that way"; for Mark Jarman, the Holy Sonnets of John Donne offered both precedent and form for poems of religious crisis. For Debra Allbery, it was the art of Vermeer that invited the private mind, "contemplation that believes itself unobserved"; for Gabrielle Calvocoressi, it was long listening to John Coltrane to find out "what it is that draws me to him" and—no longer playing the saxophone herself—to find in language "how to be the horn again."

And poems are born not only out of what is found but also out of what is fended off. As Dana Levin, refusing traditional elegy because of the consoling feelings it offered, says: "turning from elegy left me formally restless; in aversion I found invention." Chris Forhan, revoking the causal and logical connectives, banning *because, although, unless, however,* found "the new syntax . . . acting as a pickaxe, striking the hard ground of my consciousness and causing experiences, long buried but still alive, to bubble to the surface." Alan Shapiro, on the other hand, stripped away the personal, shifting the lens by limiting his scenes to public spaces seen at night and without people, seeking indirect insight through "ways of inhabiting emptiness."

Several poets give us examples of revision: Carl Dennis reveals what a change in vantage from dramatic monologue to a third-person limited point of view can accomplish in bringing a poem to convincing life; Brooks Haxton shows a poem's unplanned, even unnoticed evolution—eventually coming down, quite literally, to earth; Joan Aleshire's revision shows the illuminating power of excision.

Formal choices are often the releasing devices in poems, the way that the numbers for a lock will open the door to hidden things. A poem need not be traditionally formal, but all poems are formed; even ambiguity—the Boo Radley of any poem—has its reasons for being. Free verse calls forth its own musics: for Elizabeth Arnold, expressive meaning is served by intuitive patterns of sound—the internal echoes of rhyme, variation in duration of words; for James Longenbach, a longer, more syntactically complete line invited "a romance with information" and ultimately the insight that came of it. For Ellen Bryant Voigt, dropping punctuation and letting longer units of syntax combine and flow across the lines released a recognizable but radically reinvented free-ranging voice and vision; for Stuart Dischell, wanting "to cool hot thoughts through craft," nineteen-line stanzas "created a structure that might contain in its rhythms the stages of heartbreak—from mania to despondency."

Analyzing her poems, Betty Adcock shows us how an older form, terza rima, can haunt a looser one; "I play by ear," she says about the way patterns turn up of which she was unaware when writing and, under them, suggested meanings. That unplanned patterns emerge is one of the connective surprises of our art, as when Martha Rhodes describes how she has so far produced book-length sequences of linked poems, though she had "never set out to write a poetic sequence;" while Laura Kasischke found herself rather suddenly, and happily, writing prose poems, a form she had never liked and had always avoided. And C. Dale Young discovers, to his own surprise, the continuity of concerns in poems written over a twenty-year period.

Together, what these widely varied commentaries reveal is the exciting, unpredictable, always provisional nature of the writing process. Students and teachers of poetry can find here a variety of ways into poetic composition that we hope are instructive rather than being didactic or prescriptive. We mean instructive not in the conventional "how to" sense of most guides, but rather to suggest some of the manifold ways to subvert habit, intention, and expectation, to catch ourselves off guard, in order for the imagination to instruct us and the unforeseen to emerge. Because all of the poets in this collection, however many years we have been writing, are still in the lifelong process of learning the art and craft of poetry.

The principle of selection of these particular poets was their presence on the faculty of the MFA Program for Writers at Warren Wilson College at least twice in the last ten years. One of the great pleasures and riches of the program is this sharing of process, of craft analysis, with each other and our students—a pleasure we wish to share here with a wider audience. The low-residency program was founded in 1976, an original paradigm for graduate writing study, and since 1981 has been based at Warren Wilson College in the mountains of North Carolina near Asheville and has become the distinguished model for such programs nationwide. We thank the contributors for donating their work to this volume, whose royalties will be used for scholarships to the program.

Tony Hoagland

How I Escaped from the Autobiographical Narrative of Crisis and Resolution and Discovered Oscar Wilde and the Tradition of Theatrical Repartee

A TORTURED TALE OF PSYCHIATRY AND MAKEUP TIPS

A philosophical poet, that's what I wanted to be—a concept juggler, something along the line of Wallace Stevens. I had visions I wanted to communicate. What they were, I no longer can entirely recall.

But no one understood the poems I wrote. Words scattered around the page, congested as a head cold, here; neo-ideas, rife with noncontext, there. What is the adjectival form of *oblivion?* The response I got from my odd few readers had the flavor of polite encouragement based on the premise that poetry is allowed to be shapeless, like a raccoon in a burlap sack.

Then one day, in Tucson, Arizona, after I had been writing and reading for five or eight years, I accidentally turned three metaphors into a sort of story. My poem was lucid! And so I drifted pragmatically toward narrative structure, driven to shore by default. It turns out that I *needed* story, landscape, causality, and a time signature to make a poem; I did not have much interest in stories, really, especially my own, but I had learned that if I put a car and a stop sign and a moon into a poem, people could pay attention.

Narrative: "When X happened, I felt Y; then W happened, and I understood F." Such elementary concessions gave my poems what the movie people call a "through-line." It was a big breakthrough for me.

It's true, these narratives used the first-person singular pronoun, looked like autobiography, bore a strong resemblance to products of the Confessional era that had just passed. They tried to generate an escalating emotional pressure. I was just happy to write a poem that more or less worked.

But I had a slightly faux feeling about those narratives. I felt counterfeit, like a narrative impersonator. The narratives themselves seemed secondary to me. Narrative was just the tree on which I was hanging my real linguistic stock-in-trade: jokes, images, and metaphor. That "ornament," which may have seemed secondary to the narratives, was primary for me.

I guess a typical example of such a poem is "My Country" from my first book, *Sweet Ruin:*

MY COUNTRY

When I think of what I know about America,
I think of kissing my best friend's wife,
in the parking lot of the zoo one afternoon,

just over the wall from the lion's cage.
One minute making small talk, the next
my face was moving down to meet her

wet and open, upturned mouth. It was a kind of patriotic act,
pledging our allegiance to the pleasure
and not the consequence, crossing over the border

of what we were supposed to do,
burning our bridges and making our bed
to an orchestra of screaming birds

and the smell of elephant manure. Over her shoulder
I could see the sun, burning palely in the winter sky
and I thought about my friend, who always tries

to see the good in situations—how an innocence
like that shouldn't be betrayed.
Then she took my lower lip between her teeth,

I slipped my hand inside her shirt and felt
my principles blinking out behind me
like streetlights in a town where I had never

lived, to which I intended never
to return. And who was left to speak of what had happened?
And who would ever be brave, or lonely,

or free enough to ask?

"My Country" is an extended act of analogy, with a bunch of extra images
and metaphors thrown in for good measure. The imaginative fireworks are yoked
to a political notion, but it would be difficult for me to say which is the corpus
and which is the appendage. If the poetry customs agent looked me in the face
and said, "And what is the purpose of your trip, Mr. Hoagland—business or
pleasure?" what would I tell him? "I wanted to liken undressing a woman to the
invasion of a country; and manifest destiny to betrayal of friendship"?

Years later, when I read the poems of Larry Levis, I recognized a similar
hocus-pocus; he too was a "figurative thinker," and he made the opportunity
for that "thinking" by appending metaphor to narratives. Levis's narratives seem
mostly a matter of convenience—they are usually less original than the imagination attached to them. The conclusion of my poem above ("And who . . . ?"),
which thrilled me with its profundity when I wrote it, now seems tacked on,
self-important, and unearned. The metaphors in the poem, however, and some
of the details, seem like the candy of creativity to me; they are still fresh, and
edible.

Narrative suited me in many ways, with its mounting dramatic pressure. I
still like the sensational car-crash intensity of it. Good thing, because I would
be stuck with it for a long time.

Ten years later, though, I had painted myself into a corner. "The autobiographical narrative of crisis and resolution," as I now referred to it, seemed to lack
credibility in a number of ways. Aesthetically, it seemed so post-Confessional,
so generic and compulsory in premise. What is more, the therapeutic model
that underlies Confessionalism (crisis/insight/breakthrough) no longer seemed
TRUE to my experience. I had had plenty of crises, a lot of confusion, a little
misfortune, lots of insights. I had survived them, but what I learned under emergency conditions did NOT change my life or transform my character. Insights
were not permanent, I learned, nor were they often life-altering. The poem that
promises breakthrough was false.

After my second book I knew that I needed to find a new formal paradigm,
a different kind of poem. What else could I do?

So, for about two years, I gave up trying to write complete poems and simply filled pages with interesting lines and language, spoken by some imaginary speaker. My only criterion was that it be interesting on some level—verbally, conceptually, syntactically, tonally, or rhetorically. And I found that I *could* write an interesting sentence, attached to nothing else. With such a minimal requirement—to write an interesting sequence of words—I could manufacture the talk of characters, not of self. The mode was essentially theatrical. My goal was to amuse myself with language. The characters were invented by what they said. In that way, for me, that period of play was a kind of pure poetry.

Anyway, it was an especially happy period of time in my life: I was in love with Kathleen, I was healthy after a long period of sickness, I had a real job, and life was sweet, even if I couldn't write good poetry.

Sometimes I would fit a few lines together into a sketchy scene. My imagined model for poetry was a bitchy cocktail party with a lot of people trading repartee—vivid, wild, but aimed at no end, no resolution, no final trump card of meaning. And, importantly, on the scale of metaphysical veracity: in these "poems," every speaker gets to sound off—but no one *wins*. No one speaker owned the Truth; I didn't have to tell a story that was "mine" or that extracted drama from the use of the "I," because the dialectical multiple speakers and their remarks *were* a story. In such a scene, competing truths could be lofted without pretending that one was the final exclusive truth. The different lines were more like alternating, nonexclusive angles on actuality.

One of my more successful early exercises in multiple speakers turned into a poem called "Commercial for a Summer Night":

> We were drinking beer with the sound off,
> watching the figures on the screen—
> the bony blonds, the lean-jawed guys
> who decorate the perfume and the cars—
>
> the pretty ones
> the merchandise is wearing this year.
> Alex said,
>
> I wish they made a shooting gallery
> using people like that.
> Greg said, That woman has a PhD in Face.

Then we saw a preview for a movie
about a movie star who
is having a movie made about her,
and Boz said, This country is getting stupider every year . . .

So I had found, at least, a way of writing that could entertain me and enlarge or alter the arena of the poem from the narrative.

Employing this different method also shifted my perception of craft, from Image toward the poetic device of Tone. Now that tone was a more primary element in my work, I recognized that I had been interested in it for a long time without even noticing. *How* a thing is being said, it turns out, is a crucial part of *what*. Tone insinuates volumes of experience without requiring the testimonials of narrative. As Marianne Moore says, "Superior people never make long visits, / have to be shown Longfellow's grave / or the glass flowers at Harvard."

Another large benefit to this new poetic method was that, freed from narrative obligations, or at least, from personal narrative, my poems could include all kinds of "extraneous" information. I had come to understand, after all, that identity, that life itself, was composed of concentric circle upon concentric circle of influence and fact—history, money, language, and weather. In a dialectical poem, all those ingredients could be layered in, put into a loose orbital suspension.

When I looked around the history of my reading, I found that the models and precedents for multiple "contra-dicting" speakers had been present all along. "On the Road Home," by Wallace Stevens, for example, had always been one of my favorite poems. It begins like this:

It was when I said,
"There is no such thing as the truth,"
That the grapes seemed suddenly fatter.
The fox ran out of his hole.

You . . . you said,
"There are many truths,
But they are not parts of a truth."
Then the tree, at night, began to change,

Smoking through green and smoking blue.
We were two figures in a wood.
We said we stood alone. . . . .

As so often is true of Stevens, "On the Road Home" is a comical metaphysical poem, both game and serious phenomenology. Stevens is a fiend for alternating rhetorics, a pasha of the theatrical tradition, in which rhetoric is more important than truth.

Multiple speakers, playing games of speech badminton. It makes you wonder, How much of poetic pleasure is in delay, and prolongation? Surely this is the difference between two poetic types; the poet given to truth is trying to get to the payoff as quickly as possible; then there is the other type of writer, who is languorously, playfully enjoying the prelude to arrival, because that is all there is.

It's just another secret that everyone knew but me.

Of course, one's own writing is never a complete satisfaction. There are always glaring deficiencies and so much more to learn. So many remarkable poems to learn it from. As we get older as writers, we find our pleasure and curiosity in new places—if we lose some flexibility, perhaps we gain strategic skills, or we are better able to put old wine in new skins, or to see what we were aiming at all along. Every traveler is different, I suppose. Oscar Wilde may have died unhappy and written the (memorable, if melodramatic) line "Each man kills the thing he loves" in his poem "The Ballad of Reading Gaol." Bad news! But he gave himself and us so much pleasure when he wrote page after page of dialogue like these lines in *The Importance of Being Earnest*:

ALGERNON. Did you hear what I was playing, Lane?

LANE. I didn't think it polite to listen, sir.

ALGERNON. I'm sorry for that, for your sake. I don't play accurately—any one can play accurately—but I play with wonderful expression. As far as the piano is concerned, sentiment is my forte. I keep science for Life.

LANE. Yes, sir.

ALGERNON. And, speaking of the science of Life, have you got the cucumber sandwiches cut for Lady Bracknell?

LANE. Yes, sir. [Hands them on a salver.]

ALGERNON. [Inspects them, takes two, and sits down on the sofa.] Oh! . . . by the way, Lane, I see from your book that on Thursday night, when Lord Shoreman and Mr. Worthing were dining with me, eight bottles of champagne are entered as having been consumed.

LANE. Yes, sir; eight bottles and a pint.

ALGERNON. Why is it that at a bachelor's establishment the servants invariably drink the champagne? I ask merely for information.

LANE. I attribute it to the superior quality of the wine, sir. I have often observed that in married households the champagne is rarely of a first-rate brand.

ALGERNON. Good heavens! Is marriage so demoralising as that?

LANE. I believe it IS a very pleasant state, sir. I have had very little experience of it myself up to the present. I have only been married once. That was in consequence of a misunderstanding between myself and a young person.

My long, slow apprenticeship as a poet was, I see now, "a misunderstanding between myself and a young person." Thank goodness I am done with that! I'm happy now to be married to poetry for the time being, drinking even inferior champagne. And I try to remember that accuracy is not the point.

SUMMER SNIPER

God moves mysterious thunderheads over the towns and office buildings,
cracks them open like raw eggs. The north has critical humidity.
The south plucks at its sweaty clothes. The weatherman says it's August,
and a sniper is haunting Washington DC.

He's picking victims at random from shopping malls and parking lots,
touching them with bullets like blue fingertips,
and some say he's an unemployed geek with a chip on his shoulder,
and some say he's an agent of ancient Greek theology.

Gibb says the sniper is a surrealist travel agent
                    booking departures only
Or he's a dada lawyer without a client
                    arguing in thirty-caliber sentences.

Robin says the sniper is what the country invented
                    as a symptom of its mental illness
and Marcia is sad because she knows the sniper could have been cured
by a regimen of vitamins and serotonin reuptake inhibitors.

We had fallen into one of our periodic comas
         of obesity and celebrity
when the sniper went off like an alarm clock

and the preacher on TV
said that he had come according to Revelation 3:14

to punish us for the crime of not being ready for death—
but as Snoopy the clerk at the 7-11 said,
What kind of crime is that?

Meanwhile the air-conditioners are working overtime,
the rooftops are full of SWAT teams and camera crews
and the sky too is mobilizing:
dark clouds without speaking, menacing millennial clouds.

We don't know yet what the metaphysical facts are;
we don't know if our sniper is domestic or foreign terror,
what color the chip on his shoulder is
or what we will do if the sniper chooses us tomorrow.

But when we go out now, we feel our nakedness.
Each step has a slender string attached.
And when we move, we move more quietly,
as we slide between the sinners and the snipers

and the summer,
in the simmering medicinal rain.

WHEN DEAN YOUNG TALKS ABOUT WINE

The worm thrashes when it enters the tequila
The grape cries out in the wine vat crusher
The vine bleeds when the knife cuts through the stem

but when Dean Young talks about wine, his voice is strangely calm.
Yet it seems that wine is rarely mentioned.

He says, Great first chapter but no plot.
He says, Long runway, short flight.
He says, This one never had a secret.
He says, You can't wear stripes with that.

He squints as if recalling his childhood in France.
He purses his lips and shakes his head at the glass.

Eighty-four was a naughty year, he says,
and for a second I worry that California has turned him
into a sushi eater in a cravat.

Then he says,
              This one makes clear the difference
between a thoughtless remark
and an unwarranted intrusion.

Then he says, In this one the pacific last light of afternoon
stains the wings of the seagull pink
              at the very edge of the postcard.

But where is the Cabernet of rent checks and asthma medication?
Where is the Burgundy of orthopedic shoes?
Where is the Chablis of skinned knees and jelly sandwiches?
with the aftertaste of cruel Little League coaches?
and the undertone of rusty stationwagon?

His mouth is purple as if from his own ventricle
he had drunk.
He sways like a fishing rod.

When a beast is hurt it roars in incomprehension.
When a bird is hurt it huddles in its nest.

But when a man is hurt,
              he makes himself an expert.
Then he stands there with a glass in his hand
staring into nothing
              as if he was forming an opinion.

David Baker

Spill

THE SPRING EPHEMERALS

Here she comes with her face to be kissed. Here she comes
lugging two plastic sacks looped over her arms and stuffed

with fresh shoots. It's barely dawn. She's been out
for an hour already, digging up what she can save

before developers raze the day's lot sites and set woodpiles
ablaze. That's their plan for the ninety-plus acres.

She squats in the sun to show me wild phlox
in pink-running-to-blue, rue anemone, masses

of colt's foot, wild ginger, blood root and may-
apples, bracken and fiddlehead fern—ferns being not

spring ephemerals per se, but imperiled by road graders
come to shave the shaded slopes where they grow.

Once I held her in a snow cover of sheets. Wind beat
the world while we listened. Her back was a sail,

unfurling. She wanted me to touch stitches there,
little scabs, where doctors had sliced the sick cells

and cauterized her skin for safety's sake.
Now her hands are spotted by briars, bubbles of blood

daubed in brown. She's got burrs in her red hair.
Both sleeves are torn. She kneels as the sunlight

cuts through pine needles above us, casting a grid
like the plats the surveyors use. It's the irony

of every cell: that it divides to multiply.
This way the greedy have bought up the land

behind ours to parcel for resale at twenty-
fold what they paid weeks ago.

It's a race to outrun their gas cans and matches,
to line the path to our creek with transplants

of spice bush, yellow fawn lily, to set aside space
in the garden for the frail. She adjusts the map

she's drawn of the tumbling woods—where each
flower and fern come from, under what tree, beside

which ridge. Dysfunctional junctional nevus:
a name like a bad joke for the growth on her skin,

pigment too pale for much sunlight. *Drooping trillium,*
she says, handing me a cluster of roots, unfolding leaves—

rare around here. How delicate, a trillium,
whose oils are food for ants, whose sessile leaves are

palm-sized, tripartite. They spread a shadow over
each stem's fragile one bloom, white in most cases,

though this one's maroon. This makes it rarer.
It hangs like a red bell safe from the sun. It bends

like our necks bend, not in grief, not prayer,
as we work with our backs to the trees, as they burn.

HUNGRY

This time the jay, fat as a boot, bluer
than sky gone blue now that the rain has
finished with us for a while, this loud jay
at the neck of the black walnut keeps cawing
I want, I want—but can't finish his clause.
Hard runoff has spread the driveway with seeds,
green talcum, the sex of things, packed
like plaster against shutters and tool boxes,
sides of the barn, while the force of water
pouring down from the stopped-up gullet
of gutter has drilled holes deep in the mud.
Yet the world of the neighborhood is still just
the world. So much, so much. Like the bulldog
next door, choking itself on a chain
to guard the yard of the one who starves it.

TOO MANY

my neighbors
say, when what they mean
        are deer—the foragers, the few at a time, fair

if little more
than rats, according to
        a farmer friend nearby, whose corn means plenty.

They nip the peaches,
and one bite ruins;
        hazard every road with their running-

into-headlights-

not-away; a
        menace; plague; something should be done.

   Or here in town,
where I've
        found a kind of afterlife—the townies hate

the damage to their varie-
gated hostas,
        shadeside ferns—what they do inside white bunkers of

the county's one good
course is "criminal,"
        deep scuffs through the sand—that's one thing—but

lush piles of polished-
olive-droppings, hoof-
        ruts in the chemically- and color-enriched greens . . .

   Yet here's
one more, curled
        like a tan seashell not a foot from my blade, just-

come-to-the-
world fawn, speckled,
        wet as a trout, which I didn't see, hacking back

brush beneath my tulip
poplar—it's not afraid,
        mews like a kitten, can't walk—there are so many, too

many of us,
the world keeps saying,
        and the world keeps making—this makes no sense—
                more.

I wanted to write a love poem. I thought I would capture a moment when my wife Ann was gardening. She loves to garden and is so good she has a stall at the local farmer's market.

We had a huge garden, over two thousand square feet, with twelve twenty-foot-long raised beds, and we tended our ten acres of old woods and paths and meadows and ancient bramble. On three sides of our little acreage stretched hundreds of acres of farmland—corn and soybeans and grassy pasture—and old-growth woods of beech and oak, papaw and walnut and locust, and the thousands of smaller plants in the shade and understory.

So "The Spring Ephemerals" began like a garden, gridded, measured, carefully lined and contained. I thought it should be in quatrains, five or six of them, in decasyllabic lines. I had no title yet when the opening came: "Here she comes now with her face to be kissed. / Here she comes with an armload of baskets. . . ." What is an armload of baskets? I started to revise.

Oops, we say, sorry. Then we clean up the spill with a paper towel, maybe a mop. It's Day 83. British Petroleum spilled oil in the Gulf of Mexico, forty miles off the Louisiana coast, and it's still spilling underneath a huge rig called Deepwater Horizon. *Such a lyrical name, full of majesty and resonance—an expansive promise extending both outward and up-and-down. On April 20, 2010, eleven people died in the explosion of BP's* Deepwater Horizon *floating rig, seventeen others were badly hurt, and as far as we can guess, about five million barrels of oil have spewed, each day, a mile deep into the rich blue-black waters of the Gulf. I hope, by the time you read these words, the spill is stopped. The damage will continue for decades.*

Before I knew it, my poem about gardening spilled over. We found out that developers had their own designs for the land around us. Four hundred acres would be turned into a series of exurban neighborhoods with their McMansions, as we call them. So first Ann, then both of us, dug and replanted frantically. Like spies we sneaked onto other properties to retrieve the ferns and trout lily, twinleaf and Dutchman's breeches, before they were bulldozed. As I revised, I folded into my tidy pastoral this sudden storm of the damaged and sorrowing. I thought more about growth, appetite, and I watched my skin-cancer-susceptible wife work in the hard sun with a set jaw of determination, saving as many as she could of the small ones. I kept on revising.

Spill, a transitive verb, reaches up from the depths of Old English spillan, *which derives from older Old English* spildan: *to destroy; and bubbles up from the deep-dark Greek* sphallein, *to cause to fall. Spill, in its oldest English usage, is to kill, destroy; to cause blood to be lost by wounding. It is to allow, often unintentionally, something to fall, flow, or run out until it's lost or wasted. It is to throw off, as from a horse; to divulge, as a secret; to flow, seep, run, become scattered; to spread profusely beyond usual bounds, as a crowd into the streets.*

We can spill our guts. We can confess, blurt, blab. We spill the beans. Oops. We spill the oil.

There are dozens of houses plopped now in the middle of their one-acre plots. Most of the old trees are gone, the fewer new ones set into decorative designs. Some of the ephemeral plants we moved are still alive on the ten acres, moved to new sites along the creek and under the trees; and the creek still flows, but in its diverted bed. The water table is lower, and who knows what runoff goes where. And now, even, the long marriage is over. But the relationship goes on, and the incessant growth and spillover of things go on. I wanted the poem to face the complexity of the growth of things, the love and custody, the fear and loss, so the poem grew and grew—outsized, long lined, heavily enjambed, added-on-to beyond the bounds I had in mind. My love poem became something I had no sight of when I started. Art is full of accidents.

Tell all the truth, as Emily Dickinson advises, but tell it slant. Tell all the truth, we might say as well, but tell it deep. Tell all the truth, we might add, but sometimes let it spill. Spill . . . a mistake, an accident. Error is the heart of metaphor.

Flash forward. For four years I have lived in the village center of Granville, Ohio, population 3,200 in four square miles. As I reside here longer, and become a neighbor and citizen, one of the village people, I write about this new environment as I learn its particularities. And yes, we never quite fit. Things spill and overpower us. We feel the pressure of what we can never control. That's the heart of "Hungry," which began as a decasyllabic sonnet but grew a bit, a poem with real spilling.

Is there something useful—in fact is there something inevitable—in the making of art that we may learn from accident? Are we open, as we write, to the surprising spillover from the subconscious, from play, from association, from contradiction and interruption, from error? Some days I write to find out what I have to say. Not what I thought I would say, but what, in the process of discovery and linkage, error and spillage, I have to say. I find my poems affected, as I write, by my own daily spills and damages, those nearby, those I inhabit, and sometimes those I cause. We ruin our home even as we build it. My personal Deepwater is regional and ecological, my awareness and witness of the relation of the green world—what we used to call nature—with the peopled world. One of poetry's important tasks is to make room and include the things that often surprise us in their unbidden presence.

"Too Many" is the most recent of these poems. Its lines bear some of the weight from the work of accommodation, of making things fit or find room. Things are too crowded, aren't they? Everywhere this crowding spills over. I hope the form shows this pressure—things broken, bitten off, or overfull, unbalanced—even as I try to make something shapely and pattern-holding. Pattern out of apparent chaos: fractal as poetic form. You can probably detect a ghost of the original decasyllabic design in the opening lines.

I hope the voice of the poem finds its way to shift and reconstitute, too. It sounds to me fairly separate at first—the knowing self amid those amusing neighbors—and quick to judge. I hope it sees itself thus, too, and reorients itself. For all the blurred and plural shapes, the overplenty of deer and development, the overplenty of menace and money and leisure, there is one small figure of the fawn. What to do in this case but stop? That's the purpose behind the shift in point of view at the poem's end. The "they" becomes the "we" . . . even as the final line spills over, too long for the page, too long for the form, too long for its own good. Oops.

The wild woods are going away. Decorative engineered trees teeter among our houses and skyscrapers. The hills are smoothed off, and the creeks retrenched, and the drainage managed, the birds fewer, the animals fleeing farther back into the woods and shadows and deeper waters, while a few turn tame from our hot-house hostas and garbage dumps. The marriage is over. The oil flows. Old fires burn still belowground, and the heart grows a new vein. The world keeps making more. What can we do?

Ebb and flow. Spill and capture. Listen and sing.

Marianne Boruch

Cadaver, Speak to Me

SELECTIONS FROM "CADAVER, SPEAK"

The body—before they opened me—the darkest dark

must live in there. Where color is wasted.
Because I hear them look:
bright green of gall bladder, shocked yellow fat, acreage
flat out under skin. To think I brought this
on myself.

No blood in the lab. No longer
my blood, paste flaking
brown to the touch, the heart packed with it.
They do that too.
                    Let it pass, my husband said, for years.

But you know what? It's more, it's how
there is no sleep. It's how words
come apart in a dream.
And then you're awake.

Pale nerve, bluest black veins. Muscle gone gray
but still pink in places,
fanned out or narrowed, tendon-strict,
white elastic to knob of femur,
humerus. How on earth

to tell this. That they see things hardly
anyone. . . . Things buried, doing
for a lifetime. Sunken
            bonehouse—what body, my slow mineral ruin.

Darkness at the start. It sticks,
it bothers me: why any color at all?
Room of echo and stink. The silence we contain, we
cadavers now, water
that dumb and overflowing.
                        Blessed those—

too young to be stricken. They're kids,
in their 20s. They stare, they keep probing. To idle
amazement, to trespass like that.

Is it brave? What's *brave?* You know

then you unknow. My God, how they walk into this place
to begin with—all the ways in the smart ones, this
must burn

right through them:
                    Pure Spirit, stupid me good, just to stand here.

6.

What to hate most: this mummy way they've
wrapped our heads, thick wet towels
close, in orbit. Or the distant shock of it

I half love. The pretense that
they've blinded us. So they can work, of course,
without our staring back. *Work*—
first taking down and out the rest of us
gristle by gristle, siphon to sprocket, their silver probes
in those empty bits, all new words—my *fossa*—
is it *fossi?*—where the edge

of bony things once fit. Only they see
what's pooled there.

But it galls me—that even my dismemberment's
so predictable: my back where they little-windowed out
my spinal cord, then the slapstick flip right-side-up to shoulder, arm,
hand, on to plot my middle kingdom: liver, spleen,
down to *possible*, my mother might have said,
shooting me that look.

Nearly a century on earth gives a person
permission to be crabby
but not an idiot. When people write, I like
sentences that turn sudden,
unexpected. But that
didn't happen to me. I gave away
then wore out my ending.

When my family talks, the usual blah blah goes on:
Generous. And such a good long run!
But I never ran,
not ever.

8.

I did go to college. Nothing fancy,
one of those normal schools. I was proud
of that, smart enough, up
from the one-room schoolhouse, the old story—
a girl off the farm,

                    sort of a rarity. It wasn't exactly.

I liked words. I liked
to read—*Aesop's Fables*, Housman. Frost by heart,
the story ones especially. I loved metaphor
though nothing's really like anything else. I loved Trollope
and Dickens. Not Jane Austen—

                    she lied. Things don't

mainly end best though there's a chance
with *better*. I taught school some. Didn't care for that, no.
You have to be bossy. You have to be
certain about stars and how words rhyme, how
dollars cartwheel up and over and again

                                    to make Johnny rich.

I just kept reading.
So what's this fellow got to say all the time? my husband said,
holding my Frost to his ear, shaking it
like a box a voice might fall out of. *You should write
your secrets too!*
            No secrets, I said. But I

thought about things alone
and eyed my girls like a scientist as they grew—
if too much sleep would make them
stupid, if their quarrels were tied to weather, a beautiful day
and its boredom until

                    the spark and flash

of one simple meanness
bloomed sharp between them, for a change.
Change means: what happens
in secret. I happened, they happened, she he it happens,
a day, then a next day.
              O to write, the way people do.

17.

The air in this lab, the thing they
talk talk talk of. I already said—
not great. And it sticks
to their scrubs and their hair.

Me, my rot at the heart of it.

Not my fault. I soaked months
to clean up. And here, every late afternoon

before I'm plastic wrapped for the night, they spray
alcohol and water and *fabric softener*
all over this
body of rags strewn out on the table, my
flag of no allegiance stripped
to its zillion bad colors between worlds.
I'm so many pieces!
But this new trick of the elements—passing
into ether. Once stars and planets
famously made from it.

So—I'm at this party, right? says the med student
Claire, *and o my god,*
I smell cadaver on me!

I'm like that now: secret,
loyal as a whiff.

                    ~

And now, here: the-never-will-be
was—Which is to say
the rest could be said by anyone, I suppose.
Past tense for *not yet*
is *oh, that,* for *today*—
last week, last month, yet another Wednesday shot.
There's spring
because of winter. Before that,
fall backed into summer where rain
linked sun like some split-second lurch in the car.
Past tense of *window*
is *close it, such weather.* Past tense of *pain*
is *sleep through the night.* Before *cut here,*
sew up, cauterize (you smell something burning?)
is *rot,* is *wound,* is *cold* then *colder.*
Before war
is war. Before peace,
more war. I waited, I worried
was my bloodless lot. I remember
the stopped heart,

and before, *nothing you'd notice.*
That *nothing* on and on, huge
and years, weighs
about nothing, like
a whistle's sweet because
it's distant.
So many meant well, telling me *God*—
God this, *God* that—like
they know. Well, I never knew.
There's the body, there *was*
a body: what they found in me
in that lab
is proof. Past tense of *me*, by the way,
is *she*, a woman who lived—where
was that street?—who worked
on the farm, at school, in the dirt, at a desk,
in the shade; who read, who forgot
what she read; who drove home
after so many deaths too fast, too slow,
the last corner, the house we once
and once I wouldn't
get out of the car. *She*
who played not one instrument, even badly.
Past tense of past drifts
into ruin or myth or
did-it-happen-at-all. I won't even ask. I dreamt
same as you do. I did.

In the fall, 2008, I was given the privilege of participating in Gross Human Anatomy, a class for first-year students in Indiana University's medical school, its branch at Purdue, where I teach in the English Department. I also took life drawing, both courses the result of a "Faculty Fellowship in the Study of a Second Discipline," to put myself into the strangest situation, just to see what would happen. The award was lucky and troubling, especially the go-ahead nod to be a loose cannon in the so-called cadaver lab. I dutifully slipped into the blue scrubs and lab coat they issued me and tried for the calm and x-ray vision required.

Every day after class, I did what I've never done: wrote in a journal. At home (and not exactly in the "tranquility" Wordsworth advised), I elaborated on all I'd observed among the unnerving sights, scents, and sounds around the four cadavers, the center of our focus. I had no idea what might come of these images. Eventually a sequence of thirty-two poems—"Cadaver, Speak"—launched me into a new way to work with and beyond my usual "begging bowl" method of going blank then taking up whatever wandered to mind. It turned out to be far more willful, given the vast amount of *stuff* involved.

That spring, the poems began. The observer in the cadaver lab—some standardized version of me, of course—eked automatically into the voice, to hold forth. But really, who's the star then? It got old—fast—the poet/speaker ultrathinking yet again: elevated, self-absorbed unto unctuous, no chance for genuine discovery. I've rarely trusted persona poems. Still, I'd been drawn to, most moved by, the oldest cadaver who was as small as my grandmother had been small; that stranger curled on her side seemed to sleep the same way as she did. This dismantling of fellow humans to train doctors—well, that's the thing. But what about me, dumbfounded, a clear imposter in my real lab coat? The pure gall of it. Even my favorite cadaver would have disdained, not liked me at all, I was sure. In any case, I saw the same/old, same/old *I am the poet and you're not* creeping into those early few pieces, its know-it-all rush which is, alas, rarely a rush.

The change in my process turned sharply, on one word. The original version led off with this sentence: "The body—before they opened her—the darkest dark / must live in there." I read and reread; my cadaver, her once-among-us very lively indeed, close, wanting in. I suddenly *heard* that too—"before they opened. . . ."—*me*, yes!—"before they opened me"—*her* wonder, not mine, at what mysteries would befall her in the lab, the cadaver herself talking. It scared me, not to death, but certainly that jolt would keep this going for real because at last—a chance to be curious. Let *her* think thoughts. I, who knew nothing, had no clue. My begging bowl come back!

We write to find out. The sequence took shape, pretty much a flood then, poem after poem, bits of life I kept overhearing, the remembered and the imagined. Though I was never told anything beyond her age or cause of death, she did open, unaccountably, to charm and darken me: her sorrow, her wit, how tender she was, her humility, her steel. (So that's why fiction writers fall in love with their characters and don't want to leave them, even to eat supper . . .)

Try for *invisible*, I told myself, which must mean *tactful*, go empty as possible.

Michael Collier

The Pressure of Reality

AN INDIVIDUAL HISTORY

This was before the time of lithium and Zoloft
before mood stabilizers and anxiolytics
and almost all the psychotropic drugs, but not before thorazine,
which the suicide O'Laughlin called "handcuffs for the mind."
It was before, during, and after the time of atomic fallout,
Auschwitz, the Nakba, DDT, and you could take water cures,
find solace in quarantines, participate in shunnings,
or stand at Lourdes among the canes and crutches.
It was when the March of Time kept taking off its boots.
Fridays when families prayed the Living Rosary
to neutralize communists with prayer.
When electroshock was electrocution
and hammers recognized the purpose of a nail.
And so, if you were as crazy as my maternal grandmother was then
you might make the pilgrimage she did through the wards
of state and private institutions,
and make of your own body a nail for pounding, its head
sunk past quagmires, coups d'etat, and disappearances
and in this way find a place in history
among the detained and unparoled, an individual like her,
though hidden by an epoch of lean notation—"Marked
Parkinsonian tremor," "Chronic paranoid type"—
a time when the animal slowed by its fate
was excited to catch a glimpse of its tail
or feel through her skin the dulled-over joy
when for a moment her hands were still.

BINDING SPELL

The helicopter on TV
lifting from the White House lawn reminds me

of spells I recited to freeze the kidnapper or thug,
rehearsed in the day-dream space of school dismissal

or across the open lots piled with tumbled sage
and repeated like a chant inside the mind's idea of itself,

words that brought the bully to his knees
or made the slowing Rambler or Studebaker,

—the driver rolling down his window—vanish.
What saved me was the curse that bound the object to its fate,

words that filled the urn or vial of dark wishes,
what once was etched on fragments of papyrus,

lost for millennia but alive in calculations of revenge
or days of better fortune, and so I say this now:

I bind you, deceiver of the deceived.
I bind you by the tail of the snake, the mouth

of the crocodile, the horns of the ram, the poison
of the asp, the hair of the cat, and the penis of God—

so that you may never destroy again those
you have invaded, nor call yourself liberator,

you who have taken to binding others with the collar
and leash, while the dog, crazed but restrained,

yaps in the hooded face.

DOCTOR FRIENDLY

He was an example of anti-nominal determinism,
though he was friendly in manner, kindly
explaining that my light headedness
and the cold nausea moving through me
probably, most likely, was the Novocain

he'd shot twice into a vein or vessel,
instead of numbing the surrounding nerves
and tissue—and that's why my heart was racing, too—
but he could try again, though only once more,
for that was all the dose a male my weight could handle.

Maybe, sitting in the chair, blinded by the watery
examination lamp, and still feeling the heavy weight
of the x-ray bib across my chest and abdomen,
I didn't have the distance I needed to make a good decision.
It was like the time I was thrown out the door

of my van on the second or third roll, and landing
somehow conscious but not unscathed in the road,
my only thought was to sit down, right where I was,
just for a moment, to collect myself, which is precisely
what I was doing when a passerby urged me to get up

and go with him to the shoulder of the road.
And that's what I did and that's what Doctor Friendly
should have done, suggested I lie calmly in the chair,
take a minute to compose myself, and then reschedule.
What idiot, blind, fearful, un-numbed part of me

assented to the third injection, I know well,
for who can refrain from administering
the shock or current, cinching the collar, or denouncing
the illiberal rule laid down for the liberal cause?
Who can concede to better judgment and be grateful

for the stranger who leads you from the road
and stays until the cops arrive,
or wave off the final swab of numbing gel,
that brought me to the brink again
beneath Doctor Friendly's masked, inscrutable face.

THE BEES OF DEIR KIFA

The sun going down is lost in the gorge to the south,
lost in the rows of olive trees, light in the webs of their limbs.

This is the time when the thousands and thousands come home.
It is not the time for the keeper's veil and gloves,

not the time for stoking the smoker with pine needles.
It would be better to do that at midday, under a hot sun,

when the precincts are quieter; it would be better to disturb
few rather than many. At noon, the hives are like villages,

gates opened toward the sun or like small countries
carved from empires to keep the peace, each with its habits—

some ruled better by better queens, some frantic and uncertain,
some with drifting populations, others busy with robbing,

and even the wasps and hornets, the fierce invaders who have settled
among the natives, are involved in the ancient trades.

But now with the sun gone, the blue summer twilight
tinged with thyme and the silver underside of olive leaves

calm in the furrowed groves, darkening the white chunks
of limestone exposed in the tillage, the keeper in his vestments

squeezes the bellows of the smoker, blows a thin blue stream
into an entrance, loosens the top, like a box lid, and delivers more.

For a while, the hive cannot understand what it says to itself.
Now a single Babel presides in the alleys and passageways

and as block by block, the keeper takes his census,
he could go ungloved, unveiled, if it weren't for the un-pacified,

the unconfused, returning, mouths gorged with nectar,
legs orange with pollen, landing, amassing, alerting the lulled

to scale their wax trellis or find the glove's worn thumb, the hood's
broken zipper and plant the eviscerating stinger.

For Zein and Bilal El-Amine

During the first part of the last decade I was writing a series of elegies haunted by the loss of several friends who died just before and after the turn of the century. Writing under the discipline of a large but quiet grief, my poems seemed isolated from the awful events that were taking place in the world. When I came to the end of the elegies, I found that September 11, 2001, and the wars in its aftermath began to assert themselves.

"Binding Spell" appropriates language from an ancient Greek binding spell. Although I didn't realize it at the time, restraint and torture are inherent elements of these spells, and so, looking back, it's not so surprising that I was led to the image of a hooded Abu Ghraib prisoner. This image has settled as deeply and profoundly in the contemporary, collective psyche as has the image of the collapsing World Trade Center towers. And in its relationship to art and poetry, it reminds me of what Wallace Stevens says about "the imagination pressing back against the pressure of reality."

Torture and incarceration worked their way into "An Individual History" and "Doctor Friendly," as well. The speaker in "Doctor Friendly" discovers in an almost absurd way his own propensity for "administering / the shock or current, cinching the collar, or denouncing / the illiberal rule laid down for the liberal cause." And in "An Individual History," I had started out trying to write something like a found poem, using phrases from the records of the annual medical examinations my maternal grandmother was given during the four decades she was "hospitalized" in the Indiana State Asylum. I had no idea that my grandmother's plight might have some connection to the world's "quagmires," "coups d'etat," "disappearances," or the "detained" and "unparoled" of the past sixty years, anymore than I could foresee a visit to a dentist more than twenty-five years ago would occasion a poem about our ability to inflict physical pain on others.

In "The Bees of Deir Kifa," I was trying to write about an encounter I had with beekeepers I met in southern Lebanon in 2007, less than a year after the August war of 2006. One beekeeper had lost more than two hundred hives during the war, as well as his warehouse. The stories we exchanged about our bees—mine in Vermont and theirs in Lebanon—and our knowledge of the mysterious colony collapse that was happening worldwide were ways of acknowledging how we were all caught up in the forces of history, playing roles as observers and actors to various degrees. In this poem, perhaps the pressure of reality proved too much for the imagination, because what began as a poem about one of the charming and friendly beekeepers who took me in his dilapidated Mercedes to see his hives turned into something much more allegorical and sweeping.

Not all of the poems I've written in the past five or six years engage with the images and tropes of torture and incarceration generated by the geopolitical upheavals since September 11, 2001, but I've been surprised by how readily they appear and can magnetize and redirect a poem once they have broken through the initial impulse to write.

Gabrielle Calvocoressi

Transition: Some Thoughts on Pedagogy and the New Old Sound

"I've found you've got to look back at the old things and see them in a new light."
—JOHN COLTRANE

Lately I've been driving about four hours round trip to get back and forth to the classes I'm teaching. I don't mind the drive, but I did realize that I'd need a project in order to make the most of all that open, empty time. I've decided to spend the next fifteen weeks listening to the latter half of John Coltrane's catalog. Partially because I love John Coltrane and mainly because, like most things I love, I have a suspicion that I may not really know him at all. Which is to say, I may not really understand what it is that draws me to him. I want to see if I can find out.

It's a project that probably started when I was about eight and played alto saxophone. My father bought me a bunch of Coltrane vinyl so I could listen and play along. I'd sit there for hours, listening and then trying to sound just like him. Not surprisingly it never really felt like Coltrane even when I got all the notes right. I remember one day when I was thirteen I finally just let myself go and play *alongside* Coltrane instead of trying to be Coltrane. I'd learned a great deal from the years of strict imitation, I had a kind of muscle memory for those songs and their changes. I knew how the deepest notes felt inside me. Literally. There has never been another feeling in my life (save one, perhaps) that comes close to vibrating at the same frequency as my saxophone while I played. Having learned those lessons, I was now ready to be in conversation with that music. Which is to say, I was becoming an adult. That first moment of speaking my piece with that music, pushing into it and also finally hearing it, was a revelation. It is not surprising to me that soon after I began writing poems.

Which I have continued to do long after I put my saxophone down and allowed my father to sell it to the child of a friend. It's a funny thing to stop playing an instrument. I long for it, and yet I know that that longing is one of the most important muscles in my poems. How to be the horn again. How to make the reader feel that vibration in their body as if they are blowing the horn when they move through my poems. Like all great teachers, John Coltrane is my constant companion, pushing me and forcing me to question all I think I know. He surprises me and shows up when I least expect it. All through my second book he kept appearing. The song "Alabama" formed the bass line of thinking about the terror and beauty of the summer of 1964. At first it was just the melody. Then I went deeper and learned that the song, which was written in response to the killing of Denise McNair, Cynthia Wesley, Carole Robertson, and Addie Mae Collins, follows the exact intonations and pacing of Dr. King's eulogy for the four little girls. I was back in the room at the top of my house being taught about the rigor and freedom of moving from imitation to conversation.

Last week I was driving and popped Coltrane's *Transition* into the CD player. It's a complicated work. A bridge from his more traditional-sounding work into a more deeply experimental sound. I'm going to really have to work at it. In the midst of all that challenge there was the highly melodic section, "Welcome," which is so similar in its changes to "Alabama." I'd never realized that before and almost drove off the road in surprise and delight. There he was, about to delve into entirely new territory and using all he'd learned before to move him forward. I'm going to learn all about it. And then I'm going to say my piece.

ACKNOWLEDGMENT, 1964

Could have gone west. Could have packed your things,
who cares that you weren't old enough to drive.
Could have sold yourself to truckers
and highwaymen, could have gone down
the dark road between home and somewhere
better, the whole world watching tv and not one thinking of you.
Could've got lost. Could have said, "I don't know"
when the waitress asked, "Where you live at?"
You could have lied and said, "New Jersey"
or "Mobile." Of course, that assumes
you'd get past Mason Dixon.

You could have seen battlefields:
Gettysburg, Fredericksburg even Chicago
if you waded deep enough into summer. Could have slept
with your head on the ground like your sister,
her ear to the transistor, listening,
listening to "I Want to Hold Your Hand."
You could have said, "Fuck the Beatles"
and left them behind, shooting the lights out
of every stadium, every coliseum.

You could have made girls scream because
you were the stranger under the bleachers, that ember
of the cigarette burning in the darkness just outside their
porch lights' glow. You could have named them;
Helen, Rachelle, Ida May and in Texas *Irene Rosenberg*
a girl just as lonely as you. Imagine,

your leaving before it ever got started. *Where's that
girl you married?* You don't know. You were half way
to Billings or Provo or Bend. You watched the cities
of the Midwest burn. You threw bottles and never
cut your hair. Remember the drum kit in Schlessinger's
Instruments? How you crawled through the broken
window and banged away in the shards of that city.
If they could have seen you then! All muscle
and heart, sweating, sweating no more stupid melody
holding you back. Just the bass line, just the gas line
hissing and your foot on the pedal.

You could have gotten away. The country was different
a boy could walk without getting beaten beyond an inch
of his life, without getting lashed to a fence
in God forsaken Wyoming. Why, God hadn't forsaken
Wyoming or Birmingham yet. Chaney, Goodman
and Schwerner safe in their beds. Perhaps you passed
by them. You could have passed me by and saved yourself
the whole mess. My mother doesn't know you yet. She's
on her back in the grass with some other man's son.

A LOVE SUPREME

You beautiful, broke-
back horse of my heart. Proud,
debonair, not quite there

in the head. You current
with no river in sight.
Current as confetti

after parades. You
small-town. Italian
ice shop next to brothels

beside the highway.
Sweet and sweaty. You high
as a kite coming

down. You suburban sprawled
on the bed. You dead? Not
nearly. Not yet.

A LOVE SUPREME

Breathless in the backwoods
backlit by what joy could hold you
I see you, naked as stripped wire

all coiled against the quarry man's
hands. You dance the polecat dance
I lay by the tires, unseen. I crawled

here, sniffing the ground for clues,
bloodhound, girl child rooting you out.
Get gone, you'd say. No way ma mere.

I love you like Elvis loved pistols,
stroking you in the television light
the possibility of that music

better than all the stages in the world.
Girl, you keep rocking just like so
I'll go down river and catch you a fish

with my dirty hands, no man
can contain the love I have for you
nor the rapt attention. *Take my hand,*

take my whole life too. I've slicked
my hair back, I've made myself
a boy for you.

ROSARY CATHOLIC CHURCH

I remember the time she showed it to me. Each bead with a carving of a saint inside, chasm between robe and flesh or the hard line of a walking stick no longer than the leg of a staple. That's what faith was, something I couldn't see but felt all over. *Like a charge* she'd say. *Like when they put the wires on my head and I shook and shook.* I couldn't imagine. Most days I didn't even try. Why not play outside or bring every can in the house to the store for recycling? Much better than working the one thought over. Mother in the bed and if I looked closer Mother with the wires, thin as crickets' legs and humming already, before the music even reached. Mother glistening. Mother glowing with the spirit. All the windows of her mind blown out and the light pouring in so you can't tell the fire from the moon. And the organ straining in the heat, the groan of the instrument pushed past comfort toward the highest register. But maybe not, maybe such a low groaning that you could feel it without knowing. How hot the pipes must have gotten. Those men in their white suits stepping back from her body so as not to get caught by the current. *And this is just one day,* she'd say. *This is just one day of suffering.*

Roger Fanning

Ambiguity's Haunted House

"God Trumps Beelzebub (Among Other Bad Angels) Who Drove Me to Suicide in 2004" is, as the title says, about my one-and-only suicide attempt. I never thought I would do such a thing. I love my family. On the other hand, I was oppressed all summer by the prospect of teaching a four-hour graduate class. To prepare, I was reading *7 Types of Ambiguity* by William Empson and thinking hard about it. I was also studying *The Poetics of Indeterminacy* by Marjorie Perloff. I suppose I was depressed. I was waking up a lot at night, hearing strange noises. Twice I saw a gargoyle devil thing sitting on the peak of our roof. For some reason it reminded me of the Peter Pan ride at Disneyland, the cityscape at night. The gargoyle devil thing was looking out over the city, and I got the distinct impression it was pondering a decision. Then it turned and looked at me. Scary, but not terrifying. The night of the suicide attempt was terrifying. I had not eaten or slept for three or four days. I had a break with reality.

After that catastrophe I did not write any poems for about three years. Then I wrote "Fun." One Saturday night Kathy and Henry and I were listening to *Little Steven's Underground Garage,* a radio show, when we heard our dog Jeb barking real hard in the back yard. We went out with a flashlight and found not one but two raccoons up in a tree. A happy night. Incidentally, our dog is a coonhound, brindle with a black saddle, and his brindle fur shows up as a hospital hallucination in the first poem. I used the Terrance Hayes poem "Sonnet" as the model for "Fun."

Most of my poem "Beowoulfian Bathos of Halvor and the Trolls" is a retelling of the Norwegian folktale "The Cat on the Dovrefell." What makes the folktale funny peculiar, rather than merely funny ha ha, is the given that a gang of trolls shows up on Christmas Eve and takes over Halvor's house and Halvor has to go away for a day. There is no explanation for the arrangement. Poor Halvor. Ultimately my final poem is about anger. It is about a conscious decision to turn my anger outward rather than inward in the future.

Christopher Smart, William Blake, Theodore Roethke: these are some of my heroes. Some of their poems are visionary. I used to think it was silly when someone would talk about "taking a risk" in a poem, but I understand now there can be great psychic risks in writing certain poems. There's a risk in reading Empson's great book; you start to see ambiguity everywhere. There's a ridiculous risk in cutting your wrists. I also know there is joy in reading and writing poems that describe what other people cannot see.

GOD TRUMPS BEELZEBUB (AMONG OTHER BAD ANGELS)
WHO DROVE ME TO SUICIDE IN 2004

Chances I took with my life
when I was young: playing
in a gravel pit, driving drunk,
not using a condom. I also
drank water out of a mountain stream
once. . . .

Many years went by
prudently.

Then what?

One summer night I saw a numinous gargoyle
on the peak of our roof. He turned and stared
malevolently over his shoulder at me, a premonition of
the evil tongues, the destruction to come
(also, I could smell cowshit, though I live in a city).
Devil Ibex Horns, Batwings, the Whole Bit:
the Evil One at his Most Dramatic.
I lay very still in my bed.
I was not unimpressed.

(And now a lyrical essay about trying
to be a better person:
I used to worry about the Orangutans in Borneo.
I used to worry about the future of the rain
forest because of big bad McDonalds.
I used to listen to MURMUR over and over.

I still love the warm voice, I still love
the kudzu-crazy vacant lot, I still love the way
the album's best phrase acknowledges a passion
the opposite of most pop songs': "Get away from me."
Why then all the disillusion with R.E.M.
now? Overexposure, dilettante politics, arena rock. . . .
We all grow up and have to make money
but how much? The Buck stopped where?
Ground Zero.)

2004, the Fall following the Gargoyle Summer,
a coyote-craven frenemy of mine
(who, unbeknownst to me, wanted
to steal my wife) dosed me with LSD
on a piece of dark chocolate. Just like
that a crack spread across the van's windshield
but I enjoyed intensely the vivid orange October
foliage, the cold air, the quiet save for our
crunchy bootsteps, that hike in the mountains.
At the end of the trail the Coyote
Trickster wheeled viciously, snarling at me:
"Women cheat, she's gonna be gone."

He had already dropped by the house a couple DVDs:
PRAY FOR DEATH and FACES OF DEATH.

And yet more hatred was to come my way.

Two days after the hike the Peanuts character Linus
from the band Mountain Con got belligerent
in class, castigating me for being
a soft-spoken teacher.
He kept barking the word
"ambiguity." He would not shut up.
When he returned to his seat, he
sat there glaring at me, his chest heaving.
By that time I was insane;
nonetheless class continued.
Eventually a lumpy young woman in a trenchcoat,

Cat, made a cryptic remark
about another teacher's stuttering, or my son's
autism, or Russell Edson's essay on silence,
or all of the above:
"the handicap of language." Like I said
I had gone insane.
Perhaps Linus had lost his mind
too. Cat seemed deliberately acidic.

Three days after the hike
my life became a shrieking visual confusion
synesthesia off and on
(my brain a pet store full of electric green
parakeets panicked by a thunderstorm).

Three nights I had lain awake holding a knife.
Once I saw a sultriness: my wife crouching like a lioness
beautiful but threatening beside me in bed.

Suddenly the urge to light three candles in the bathroom.
Donald Trump, he with the redblonde rat's nest on his head,
pooched his mouth out on TV, as if pondering
the Sorcerer's Apprentice. I was frantic to get in the tub.
I was terrified two G-men in an Oldsmobile
would frogmarch me outside and put me in the trunk
and elsewhere torture secrets out of me.
They would sport blonde crewcuts
and wear latex gloves and be subtle
when it suited them, then brutal.
Goodbye, goodbye to aluminum siding.
Goodbye, son. Hello, dead parents.
I washed down all the pills I could find
and I cut both my wrists with my dead
father's trusty short sharp fishing knife
(still keen for cutting heads off trout).
Blood left me, bathwater my shadowself.
Pure opera, pure bullfight.
Thrown red roses. Bravo,
bravo middlebrows.

Then two weeks at Harborview with its intermittent
terrors and its glittery astringent smell. At night medication
made my lips so dry they flaked like fishfood, as if
I were a timelapse human sacrifice. Every morning I recalled

a grad student who had written a poem about my son
flapping his hands in the back yard.
How did that student know about my secret pain? Why
such cruelty in the duchy of dactylic
stabitty stab stab? The less

said about it to the hospital staff
the better. I stonewalled them as best
I could, as if I were a zombie POW
in a neverending horrorshow where the walls
each night get carpeted with brindle fur
and the grounds put on a pelt of diamonds. . . .

At last the powers-that-be let me go home
to my wife Kathy (affectionate, she of
the grilled cheese sandwiches and soup and sex)
and then our son Henry home from school
(a little skittish of my scars, underfed,
fat-lipped), and my life too sweet,
at least that day, to be
bedeviled or believed.

FUN

Fun to pull the fire alarm.
Fun to have no past or future.
Fun to see a dog with his ears perked up.
Fun to PITY THE BATHTUB.
Fun to discover the coelacanth.
Fun to say "bullet shit."
Fun to thunder, fun to lightning.
Fun to fork, fun to spoon.
Fun to garbanzo bean.

Fun to taste the bluewhite breastmilk.
Fun: fellatio!
Fun: cunnilingus (a little less fun).
Fun to hear sounds the deaf make during sex.
Fun to pop a bottle of bubbly.
Fun to refute Satan's sibilance.
Fun to phone.
Fun to e-mail (a little more fun).
Fun to see the Trailblazers without headbands
(I know headbands mean something bad).
Fun to thumbsdown, fun to boo.
Fun to watch Godzilla wade, dripping water.
Fun to hallucinate: a Tengu swooping out of the trees.
Fun to see Jesus on the undersides of my eyelids
(Jesus always tells you the truth).
Fun to bamboozle.
Fun to fondle the voodoo doll in the likeness of mom.
Fun to find with a flashlight the treed raccoon.

BEOWOULFIAN BATHOS OF HALVOR AND THE TROLLS

General fucked-upedness of family life,
General vacuity of advertising,
General woundedness. . . .

Great joy in exorbitant stories
because the suggestions of language, shady,
glare into commands.

Oh, those owlish fellows of All Souls college
with their index cards, descendants of
the absentmindoed moustachioed Manbeast in the Mead Hall
who looks like me, beery, boondoggled. . . .

Best of all stories:
A beautiful woman, who looks like no one else.
White skin, black hair, red lips:
Black crow, red blood, white snow.

Christmas Eve. A man is taking a white bear on a leash to the King of
Finnmark as a gift, through a forest of black sticks. The man comes to
Halvor's cabin, beside which Halvor is chopping wood.

"Can I spend the night in the cabin?"
"No, the Trolls are coming."

Nonetheless, the man sleeps standing up in a closet. The white bear sleeps
under the table. Party in full swing, party of long-nosed trolls, long-tailed
trolls, trolls all sizes, the white bear smells sausages cooking and stirs in his
sleep. White fur, a movement. Hmmm. . . . A little long-nosed troll with a
sausage on a big two-pronged fork, friendly, approaches the sleeper. "Here,
puss puss." The white bear roars out, scattering the Trolls.

A year goes by.
Halvor is chopping wood in the side yard.
A voice from the woods calls out.
"Hey, Halvor, do you still have that big cat of yours?"
"Yes, and she has seven kittens that are all much larger and more ferocious
than she is."
A pregnant silence. The Trolls never take over Halvor's house again.

How did the visits begin? I imagine
the Trolls threatened, merely by
their presence, to hurt Halvor.
What if there is one Heaven and the Trolls are there?
Imagine that: a Heaven that cannot be endured.

There's a house.
There's a wood.

Black Sticks, White Snow, No Blood.
The story would be more beautiful if there were blood.
Halvor should spill the Trolls' blood,
I would.

Chris Forhan

"Without *Although*, Without *Because*":
Syntax and Buried Memory

A decade ago, I was growing tired of my poems. They felt suspiciously tidy and knowing—even, at their worst, smug. Perhaps their ironies were necessary responses to life's confounding mysteries and paradoxes, or perhaps they were just cowardly feints and diversions. My poems were elegant little boxes that shut with a click, but I began to wonder whether something was suffocating inside them.

Then, in the summer of 2002, I wrote, quite quickly, a short poem called "Once." I liked it. It felt genuine, alive, and meaningfully strange; it felt weighty with feeling, but its meanings remained, happily, just beyond my grasp. I noticed that the poem's syntax was spare, stripped down; the poem spoke in short, declarative sentences, even fragments. There was only one conjunction, a coordinating one: *but*. There was no subordinating conjunction—no *because* or *while* or *since* or *unless*. There was no conjunctive adverb—no *however*, no *meanwhile*, no *nevertheless*.

I was surprised that the poem referred to my father, who took his own life when I was fourteen and who had been a troubling mystery for years before that. It had been a long time since I'd written so directly about him.

Then I wrote another poem, this time consciously avoiding subordinating conjunctions and conjunctive adverbs. My father showed up again. I wrote another poem; my father was in that one, too. Why was the man no longer lying silent?

The new syntax I was employing was acting as a pickaxe, striking the hard ground of my consciousness and causing experiences, long buried but still alive, to bubble to the surface. "It's about time," they seemed to be saying. This was exhilarating and terrifying: exhilarating because suddenly I was confronted by subjects I felt an urgency to write about, to interrogate and honor in poems, and terrifying because I did not understand the force that made me need to write about them—terrifying, too, because I knew now that these griefs and tumults were still within me, that I had managed to live for years without being fully conscious of them. But now I was conscious of them—simply because I had stopped saying *because.*

It makes sense that this change of syntax would lure such feelings out of hiding. The conjunctions I was avoiding signal the operations of the rational mind; they communicate judgment, discernment, a comprehension of the relationships among things. They are words we use after the fact, when we have figured something out. In forging relationships between things (because of this, *that*; after that, *this*), they imply a kind of narrative, a sequence of events in time; the absence of such conjunctions allows for utterances in which time seems to be arrested and in which multiple—even contradictory—experiences can exist simultaneously, without explanation or resolution. What is free to come rushing into a sentence, then, is not understanding but bewilderment, astonishment, anxiety, grief, and love. Those are feelings that marked my childhood and my adolescence in the aftermath of my father's death. I had allowed them to lie sleeping.

As I examine *Black Leapt In*, the book that resulted from this altered way of writing, I find only a few subordinating conjunctions—an *if* here, a *when* there. In a poem about teenage boys being at a loss for what to do with themselves, and about themselves, I mention that they are "without / although, without because." The syntax itself had become a theme of the poems.

In a way, of course, none of this is news. Hemingway understood the power of simple syntax, of conjunctions no more nuanced (or, sometimes, no less strange) in their implications than *and*. Modernist poetry as a whole is, largely, a poetry of fragments, of pieces whose authenticity is born of the artist not forcing them to fit together. But it became news to me when such fragments rose up and spoke from my own memory.

For years, I have told my students to allow a poem its meaningful mystery and complexity and to do so by repressing for as long as possible the urge to decide what their poem is about. I have told them to trust the language of the poem to help them discover that. But always I have been thinking about images, rhythms, sounds. Now I think, as well, about syntax, which led me to sense not just what a particular poem needed to be about but what I am about.

ONCE

Once, a black panic of birds scattering from a tree.
Some finger flicked them.

Once, a fox at the far edge of a field:
my father, back from battle, back with plain talk.

In lamplight, in the pages
of my math book, a gold moth.

But it was he they eased down into the dirt—
I saw it—he never recovered. Once,

rain. After, a cold sun, earthworms
in the runoff. Pharaoh hardened his heart.

TESTAMENT

Being made to drink vinegar from a sponge,
that part was true. And feeling bad for the lepers.
Being a Cub Scout with a glue gun
in a paneled den, one jar of silver glitter,
one of blue. My wings then—with duct tape
I strapped them down, near the backstop
I rolled in the dust to muss them.
The cave's mouth glowed gold but
I missed it, I was tucked in, my brain
was filled to bursting with the TV listings.
I rode a red bike with a warning bell,
I stood in the lunch line while a hole
was punched in my milk ticket. Ducks
vanished into the mist upon the wading pool—
some sorcery, some hopefulness. I lowered
my head to accept the canvas bag
of newspapers, I crossed the creaky footbridge
to Bill O'Meara's house, a pale pink light
on everything. No scribe for all that then.

A hurt squirrel pulled its bulk across the grass,
I placed my hand upon it, I washed right after.
That was not I among the reeds. I was
with the others on the patio playing Parcheesi,
I was slouched in the back of the school bus,
thumbing the transistor's volume knob.
I wore the satiny green trunks of our team.

MY FATHER'S CURRICULUM VITAE

*I was handed the pamphlet of maxims, took it into my heart, folks did that
then.*

Was grandson, pal, penitent, fulfilled the contract.

*Distinguished myself in trig and cigarettes, in whistling whatever had topped
the Hit Parade.*

*Plucked my brother from the lake, tucked him into the lining of my cap on the
chance he'd undrown one day.*

*Put on the soldier's gear, shipped island-ward, you should have seen me in my
dress whites, dozed at my post just the one time.*

Picked a gray suit and a brown one, stood rigid while the pins slipped in.

Clicked the briefcase shut open shut.

Wielded the slide rule, wielded the silver shoehorn.

Come to me, Christ, I cried, there's mud in my eye sockets.

*Woke to rustling—my dead mother, my gone father, back as two birds in a
fluster above my head.*

*Roused the children from bed, showed them how each planet spins, distant,
arranged blue marbles on the carpet.*

Dug pennies from my pocket, tossed them into a bowl.

Entered the bedroom once, ready to speak to her, sat on the floor, rocked and said nothing.

Lowered the Ford's idle, tightened the Chevy's brakes, watched the bubble fidget in the spirit level.

Whispered farewell, farewell into my own ear.

Slept late on Sundays, then Mondays, then couldn't sleep.

Knelt in a field of strawberries, damp dirt, damp leaves, pretty wife in the row to my right, my good children—

Lifted a bit of that redness to my lips, little thought in it, just taking sweetness in, sweet shock of not knowing, of not remembering. Pretty wife.

VANISHING ACT

Each bed with a child in it, or his wife,
his brain lined with sleeping bees,

my father is having to leave the house
with delicacy, easing the dead bolt open

in the dark. The house exhales him.
I'm thinking of a driving lay-up, of a girl

in homeroom, blue necklace, brown skin.
Transistor radio on my pillow, volume low.

I know some things, not enough. My eyes
are closed, I'm listening hard, that song

again, *Knock down the old gray wall,*
my father standing beside his car—gone,

key in his hand, snowflakes in his hair.
At dawn, an Indian-head test pattern will stare

from the TV, the freezer will churn out
its automatic ice. On the windowsill

an iris in a vase will have taken
the last water into its cut stem. I will

notice it, how it is there, and had
stood there the whole time, that flower.

BLACK

Sludge at the edge of the field, still water, slat fence
and its rickrack shadow. Trowel tongue.
Tulip rooted in black, cricket soaked in it.
Mask of the cedar waxwing. Snipe's eye, fly's face.
A nudge does it, if you're young enough.
My jaw dropped and black leapt in,
black spleen, black brain, black car
pulling out of the driveway, turning at the top of the hill,
then noon, black in its blue suit.

CRUISING LAKE CITY

Car full of fuckups, unlaureled easy ironists,
'twas witlack we suffered, 'twas sixteen
and Emerson, Lake, and Palmer
and inexact timing, fingers drumming the dash
and seat backs, a kind of piety in that,
Scott's mom's dilapidated Plymouth,
burger bags, bullhorn for public wisecracks
in Kurt's Pakistani accent, 'twas certitude
and love, love
like a fox that gnawed at our chests, Al
rolling his window down on Beth's block

to place in each mailbox
a tiny mustard pack, I
slouched in the back, a mistake with a face—
what fuse in Sue Cardinal's heart
had blown so it could not want me, so it would not
grieve if I kneeled and died
beneath her window, unhoused, how about that,
night fog like wool in the trees,
none of us mentioned it, rudderless
we rode, without
although, without because, just
this, this, this
and us, which was almost enough.

WHAT HE LEFT BEHIND

Jam jar of cigarette ends and ashes on his workbench,
hammer he nailed our address to a stump with,
balsawood steamship, half-finished—

is that him, waving from the stern? Well, good luck to him.
Slur of sunlight filling the backyard, August's high wattage,
white blossoming, it's a curve, it comes back. My mother

in a patio chair, leaning forward, squinting, threading
her needle again, her eye lifts to the roof, to my brother,
who stands and jerks his arm upward—he might be

insulting the sky, but he's only letting go
a bit of green, a molded plastic soldier
tied to a parachute, thin as a bread bag, it rises, it arcs

against the blue—good luck to it—my sister and I below,
heads tilted back as we stand in the grass, good
luck to all of us, still here, still in love with it.

Linda Gregerson

Going Elsewhere

PRODIGAL

Copper and ginger, the plentiful
    mass of it bound, half loosed, and
      bound again in lavish

    disregard as though such heaping up
were a thing indifferent, surfeit from
    the table of the gods, who do

    not give a thought to fairness, no,
who throw their bounty in a single
lap. The chipped enamel—blue—on her nails.

The lashes sticky with sunlight. You would
    swear she hadn't a thought in her head
    except for her buttermilk waffle and

    its just proportion of jam. But while
she laughs and chews, half singing
    with the lyrics on the radio, half

    shrugging out of her bathrobe in the
kitchen warmth, she doesn't quite
complete the last part, one of the

sleeves—as though, you'd swear, she
        couldn't be bothered—still covers
            her arm. Which means you do not

    see the cuts. Girls of an age—
fifteen for example—still bearing
        the traces of when-they-were-

        new, of when-the-breasts-had-not-
        been-thought-of, when-the-troublesome-
cleft-was-smooth, are anchored

on a faultline, it's a wonder they
        survive at all. This ginger-haired
            darling isn't one of my own, if

        own is ever the way to put it, but
I've known her since her heart could still
        be seen at work beneath

        the fontanelles. Her skin
    was almost other-worldly, touch
so silken it seemed another kind

of sight, a subtler
        boundary than obtains for all
            the rest of us, though ordinary

        mortals bear some remnant too,
consider the loved one's fine-
            grained inner arm. And so

    it's there, from wrist to
    elbow, that she cuts. She takes
her scissors to that perfect page, she's good,

she isn't stupid, she can see that we
    who are children of plenty have no
        excuse for suffering we

should be ashamed and so she is
and so she has produced this many-
    layered hieroglyphic, channels

    raw, half-healed, reopened
    before the healing gains momentum, she
has taken for her copy-text the very

cogs and wheels of time. *And as for*
    her other body, says the plainsong
        on the morning news, *the hole*

    in the ozone, the fish in the sea,
you were thinking what exactly? You
        were thinking a comfortable

    breakfast would help? I think
    I thought we'd deal with that tomorrow.
Then you'll have to think again.

HER ARGUMENT FOR THE EXISTENCE OF GOD

This one then: the
doctor, who of course possesses a foreign name, thus
                        gathering all our what
shall we call them our powers of foreboding in a single

sordid corner of
the morning news, contrived to miss the following:
                        eight fractured ribs,
three missing fingertips, infected tissue, torn and partly

healed again,
between the upper lip and gum and, this you have to use
                      your Sunday
finest to imagine, a broken back, third lumbar, which

had all
but severed the spinal chord leaving him "floppy," or so
                              the coroner later
theorized, below the waist. Now granted she might not have

thought to expect
a wailing one-and-a-half-year-old to toddle adorably
                              over the tiles nor
felt she had the leisure to apply her little mallet just below the

knee, we see that, but
we are not talking nuance here. The tooth he had swallowed, so
                              hard had been
the blow to his face, of course one had no inkling, that would

take some sort of
psychic or an MRI. But ulcerated lesions on the scalp and
                              ears? I tell you if
I hear once more how the underage mother's underage boyfriend

suffered a difficult
childhood himself I'll start to wreck the furniture. When I'm
                              allowed to run the world you'll
have to get a license just to take the course on parenting and

everyone
will fail it and good riddance we'll die out. But in the
                              meantime which
is where we're always stranded and ignoring consolation

which is laughable what's
to be made of the sheer bad fit? The reigning brilliance
                              of the genome and
the risen moon. The cell wall whose electric charge forms now

a channel now
a subtle barrier no modulating thought has thought
                              to equal. The
arachnid's exoskeleton. The human eye. And we who might

have been worthy but
for reasons forever obscure to us aren't. Wouldn't you
                    rather be damned
for cause?

Writing is a deeply paradoxical process, I find, especially when it comes to
the writing of poems. Witness the freedom-in-bondage that constitutes our basic contract with poetic form: every poet has discovered for herself the extraordinary imaginative liberation that proceeds, or can proceed when we are lucky,
from servitude to too many masters: to syntax and lineation at the very least,
to meter, rhyme, image-logic, alphabet, anaphora, refrain, story, and dramatic
voicing when we choose to take those on as well. Scrambling as best we can
with the strictures of mixed allegiance, we find ourselves too busy to overplot
the unfolding of affect and cognitive discovery. Hence that blessed ambush they
used to call the Muse.

The paradox I'd like to illustrate by means of the two poems printed above
is the one I think of as moving-forward-by-going-elsewhere. Often, when I have
drafted, oh, three-quarters of a poem, something more than half in any case, I
find myself at a peculiar sort of impasse. The trajectory has begun to assume
some clarity; the poem has begun to turn toward home. And just-on-the-edge-
of-fulfillment is exactly the problem: were the poem at this point simply to
complete its own momentum, it would land in sorry predictability or, worse,
the default didacticism that comes from "topping up" one's own emergent understanding. Time to go elsewhere, Linda. And begin by discarding that last
stanza and a half.

Elsewhere can be recalcitrant. A dozen failed efforts to find it—three
dozen—are nothing at all. It must be the right, the real elsewhere, the one that
deepens and corrects what has come before. "Prodigal" is a poem about my niece
Rebecca, whom I adore, and who had been going through a difficult time when
I wrote this poem: she had begun to cut herself, and we who love her were
distraught. Such a poem is rife with opportunities for trespass: Who was I to
violate Rebecca's privacy? Who are we, we first-world, eating-disorder- and self-
harm-riddled progeny of surfeit, to talk about suffering? Etc., etc. And so, en
route, I had littered my floor with discards, especially of the second-guessing,
poet-doth-protest-too-much variety. And had come, by steering (I'd hoped)
the narrow path between wretched error and wretched error, to what is now
the first half-line of stanza nineteen: "the very / cogs and wheels of time." The
story had been told. But the poem wasn't over. Another floorful of discards and
several days later, it hit me—the larger story of which this one was symptom.

It couldn't enter—that larger story—as part of the continuous narrative voice, lest the narrator seem to take credit for understanding she hasn't even begun to achieve. (How did I discover that? I discovered it by writing it the wrong way first.) It had to come in as disruption and undersong: a new voice that breaks the surface of the poem-so-far and a voice that is only implicit (an undersong) in the morning news. Which exposes the narrative consciousness (returning as part of what is now a dialogue) in all its inadequacy and evasion.

In "Her Argument for the Existence of God," the moment of going on by going elsewhere occurs in stanza nine. I'd launched the poem in the form of a rant—my effort to overcome the default mode to which (my own) poetic voice so easily concedes, that wishing to seem large-hearted and judicious we call ingratiation. And the rant, at "good riddance," had run its course. But where to go from there? In this case, the elsewhere that came to my rescue was a counterargument, one that precedes and staggeringly outstrips the vistas of human wreckage. Its message, of course, was not particularly cheering. But I knew it, when it hit me, for the true one, at least for this poem.

A. Van Jordan

Cinematic Movement of *Metropolis* and *Un Chien Andalou*

Writing *Metropolis* and *Un Chien Andalou* came from an effort to jumpstart the writing process after a four-year hiatus from it. The idea would be three-fold: I wanted to write some poems that moved cinematically, in whatever way I would come to define this. And I wanted to watch some of my favorite films, and I wanted to watch films I always wanted to watch. So although the approach could be justified in some intellectual way, the desire stemmed purely from desire.

A few years ago, I had lunch with my editor in New York, the late Carol Houck Smith. At that time, we talked about these poems and how it might be nice to see what would happen if I could extend the cinematic theme throughout a collection. Initially, we were talking about using a screenplay format I had employed in a few poems before. In my mind, I thought I'd approach another collection with this device at play, creating what might appear to be a book-length poem, formatted like a screenplay. The more I delved into the process, though, I became less interested in this structural device and more interested in the movement of the films I found myself watching, late into the night.

What I mean by movement is the way the transitions would take place from scene to scene. I was already conscious of what these would look like on paper, in a screenplay, but I became more curious about the directorial decisions, maybe even the editorial decision in post-production, to move from one outdoor location to an interior; to move from a high angle to a low angle; and to see one character come from one side of the screen and another character, usually a foil, enter the frame from the opposite side. All of this movement seemed to signify something subconsciously. Much in the way Lorca wanted to capture the spirit of the Andalusian guitar, I wanted to capture the energy or *duende* of this art form's movement.

With this in mind, I set out to track the camera movement in the films, scene by scene. Writing down what happened, movement wise, from one scene to the next. Afterward, I would choose a scene or two as a "writing prompt," and I'd trace that movement in the poem. That is to say, if the scene opened with an aerial establishment shot outside and moved into an interior master shot, this movement would be mimicked in the poem. If this changed later in my own editing process, this was fine; I simply used the camera movement in the film as a prompt for the movement in the poem. I did maintain a sense of what came before, by way of action and image, and what came after in action and image, line by line. This is nothing new in itself, but instead of thinking of this in the sense of "I am editing a poem now," I thought of it as "if this image follows this image, and if this image comes before this image, do I have a new image?" Like in an Avid-editing suite, I wanted to know what happened when one image was wedged between two others. In the sequencing of poems, I'm conscious of what happens when one poem follows or precedes another, but I often need training wheels on when it comes to the process of thinking of image or action following in sequence within the poem. There are so many issues to keep clear all at once that it becomes a bit chaotic: the image within the syntax, the syntax draped over the line, the meter within a line. I can only think of these things later, in the revision process, but I can think within the scene, so to speak, earlier on in the process, which is what I did with these two poems.

As the title indicates, I got to see *Metropolis* with two poet friends in downtown Ann Arbor at the beautiful Michigan Theater. At the time, I was fascinated with how the movie felt more like a performance: a live organist in tuxedo tails; an introduction on the history of *Metropolis* by a film scholar; because the line was around the block outside, the delay of the show to accommodate the crowd and to get everyone seated. The theater in which I watched it opened its doors to the public on January 5, 1928, shortly after the original *Metropolis* was released, January 10, 1927. I couldn't help but think that the theater must have carried much of the same energy in the 1920s as it did that night. I was surprised that this twenty-first-century audience didn't get too fidgety sitting for two and a half hours, reading title cards and watching—albeit, stunningly composed—a black and white film. If anyone got up to go to the bathroom, you could see them scurrying back to their seats. People would let them back into their row, but the other viewer kept her eyes on the film as they made room for the returning viewer to get into the seat. People were rapt with attention, much more so than if they were watching an action film in 3D. What poet wouldn't want to capture some of that energy on the page? If nothing else, I had hoped, at least, to *explain* that energy.

With *Un Chien Andalou*, my Netflix membership came in handy because I was able to pause and rewind the short sixteen-minute film many times on my laptop. Here's a film I never really understood when I saw it years ago in a film class, and I'm not sure that I get all of it now, after having seen it a number of times, but I do know what I *feel* watching it, which is more important than full comprehension sometimes. Once again, the feel of the film is what I set out to render. For a 1929, silent, experimental film, one would think that Bunuel and Dali had an Avid editor sent back in time; the edits move like most films today with a cut every two to three seconds—image, in quick tandem, after image. Urgency, desperation, mystery, and desire are all performed in the film. They all add up to a murder mystery that not only remains a mystery to me but also remains equally as satisfying. The scene I tracked in the poem is the famous opening scene in which Bunuel cuts across the eye of Simone Mareiul, the star of the film. In the filming, they achieved this by cutting the eye of an already dead calf. The disjointed chronology follows and is punctuated with a title card reading "Eight Years Later," but the opening title card reads "Once Upon a Time." As a result, the dreamlike feel of the film is established. By following the movement of the camera, I tried to capture a bit of this without the risky cliché of "Once upon a time" entering the poem. That I think of poetry as a visual art form makes the leap to cinematic poems a bit easier or justified, if nothing else. In both of these poems, they represent an experiment with trying to mimic in the poem what is seen in the film.

METROPOLIS, RESTORED EDITION, MICHIGAN THEATER, ANN ARBOR, SEPTEMBER 14, 2010

Listening to the organist play feels like eavesdropping
inside the mind of a giant, a bipolar giant
whose emotions are so fragile I want to climb
up her arm to lay my hand on her shoulder.
The screen hasn't captured the first gray glimpse of skyline
yet. Music has already enveloped the theater,
enclosing the city in a throat filled with indifference,
a city under a chiaroscuro of sunlight imagined

by those working in the depths of the metropolis—
a sort of giant, too, with some real issues to work out.
I remember watching, as a child in downtown Akron,
Wild Oscar play the organ, ascending from beneath the stage
at the Lowes Theater, long before it was re-named
the Civic Theater, and, even longer before it needed restoring
to save its life. Wild Oscar would play before the feature
or during the silent Krazy Kat shorts preceding
the main event. Like tonight, going to the movies
seemed monumental: live music, opening acts, serpentine
lines around the block. When Oscar played,
I wonder, now, if he was happy or was he
beneath the stage the whole time
like the workers in the film tonight, preserving the magic,
a magic movie goers still believe in, the way voters
and lovers do not. Like many children, I believed
I would do something with my bulbs of brilliance
once I simply grew up. Like many adults, I
stayed a child; potential hanging around like a shadow.
And every now and then, like tonight, I catch up
with my shadow self, and show up in a theater
to see a restored edition of an old film
about workers holed up in a factory for too many hours
and lovers separated, like most lovers, by their ideas.
One worker steps off line, reprieved by a brother worker,
and suddenly the sky appears, and the whole
rectilinear contraption—and I mean their lives, not just the plant—
comes tumbling down, an arcade of beliefs
in ruins. I wonder if these events will mean
anything to this audience, whose laughter rings a bit
condescending in all the queued moments of melodrama.
It's so easy to laugh at the banana peels laid before the lives of others.
It's almost sad to see how some of the young act too old
to feel naïve, no suspension of disbelief. Not me.
The movies provide my last safe playground.
Tonight, for instance, when the organist descends to play,
and the lights expire, and the projection whirrs to action,
I'm as excited as I was as a boy. When I see the organ ascend,

what am I but as dazed as the workers climbing from the depths
of the metropolis—a little disappointed, filled with questions, wondering
how will I go on with the work of my day in all that natural light?

UN CHIEN ANDALOU

Because a razor cuts across a frame of film,
I wince, squinting my eye,
and because my day needs assembly
to make sense of the scenes anyway,
making a story from some pieces of truth,
I go outside to gather those pieces.
Thousands of moments spooling out
frames of mistakes in my day.
As if anyone's to blame,
as if anyone could interpret the colliding
images, again and again, dragging
my imagination behind me,
I begin assembling.
I don't know anything, so I seek
directions, following the path
of ants from your palm, out
the apartment door to a beach.
Is this where I'm supposed to ask
if my hands on you bend
some light around shade? Maybe
I'm not ready for the answer. They say
art imitates what we can sculpt or write
or just see when we turn ourselves
inside out. I can't turn my eye away
from the sight of failure. The rain pelts rooftops.
I listen to the song, thinking
when the sun comes back,
beating down the door
in my head, I'll salvage whatever sits
still long enough for me to render,
before anyone knows what really happened.

Karen Brennan

Lyric Stories

from "The Real Enough World"

SPIDER CITY

After a while I dreamt about
            the Spider City
& when I woke up in my
            flannel pj's
the curtain flapped open
            & the sky greeted me.

Hello Karen, Hello Little Bee,
        it said which is when
I remembered the strange
        webbed sky of the Spider
City & your face in the
        middle saying Kiss Me.

BREATHLESS CITY

Every city is a little breathless,
a little behind the times,
racing to catch up, thus
gasping.

That day I wore a gray suit,
    white gloves, 1960 or so.
Some thin man approached
    & offered me $$ to
    pose in the nude.
The sun over St. Patrick's
    Cathedral like a child's
sun, all rays around
    a smiling face
& the man whose gray suit
    matched my own was
    called Ray!

    Such coincidences
occur in a city whose heart
    splits open in two shocks.
But this happened later.
& I wasn't around
though I watched it on TV.

DIETING CITY

Or Starving City. It's hard
    to tell. For one thing, it's
    dark & for another
    I feel inadequate.
My perpetual motion has
    ceased to amuse anyone here
    (I confide) even though . . .

I wore a beautiful skirt of red silk
    & when I whirled you could
    see everything—
    the river
    with its captured lights, the
    glint of bridges, the
    pock-marked Palisades,
    aflame.

So much of this is untrue.

A worm slunk in the sidewalk cracks.
An old, old woman, wreathed
        in snot,
spoke sharply: She said,
"just because you give me five dollars
don't entitle you to my life's story."

CITY OF JOKES

A man goes to a psychiatrist
        sporting a huge gash in his
        forehead, says I bit
        myself. How did you
        do that? asks the psychiatrist.
        It was easy, says the man.
        I stood on a stool.
Afterwards, I pulled out of
        the parking garage & the
        day was overcast, streets
        icy.
I drove up the hill & took
        a right. I drove by the
        drive-in coffee place &
        the brown house with the
        shutters & took a left
        & then I was home.
        I turned
on the radio at this point.
A girl with a cane made her way
        down the sidewalk.
She was a stranger,
& she was my daughter.

CITY OF DOT DOT DOT

There was a window, a drape,
     a venetian blind thickened with
     dust, an accordion sound
up from the street . . .
Your friend the author [was] inside
this which was inside that which was
once again . . .
ad nauseum . . .
contained in . . .
etc etc . . .
     Space
     shrinks & even afternoons
     which once seemed so voluminous
     have dwindled to a sad heap . . .
Little wrinkled days no longer
     unfold . . . Lawns have grown
minuscule & purposeless . . . Hairs
sprout on the female chin & buildings
formerly majestic are . . .
But I was crazy then . . .
In the fullness of each moment . . .
I walked everywhere in the gloam & sand . . .

CITY OF BASEMENTS

Of course, conducive to sleep.
Of course, musty & poorly
     organized. You wouldn't go there
     uninvited. I wouldn't invite you.
But there are chinks in the brick ceilings
     that make it seem radiant
elsewhere, which is a blessing.

& amid the rats & spider houses
I might invent something
spectacular (I almost believe).

This is all I have to say about it.
Because it is unamenable to description.
Because even now my eyes are closing.

Pity yourself, Sister.
Life is harder than you dreamed possible.

I like to write poems in series. I always think the series will turn out to be a book, but perversely they always stop short of a book—perhaps twenty (if I'm lucky) is all I get.

These poems are from a series that appeared in my book *The Real Enough World* as the title poem. At the time I thought that the real enough world more or less described the ambiance of these poems, a particular mingling of whimsy and dread mixed in with my romantic memories and the horrific present-day aftermath of 9/11. Once it was published, I was able to write a few more of these city poems, and even now I think I could go on and on with this city series.

However, these were written within a few years of 9/11 and have very much to do with my sense of New York City both before and after that catastrophe. I've always been drawn to writing about NYC, having grown up there and having a great nostalgic connection to that time when we indeed wore white gloves and took the train to Grand Central and were able to wander around fearlessly. 9/11 happened and became, in these poems, one of the ways of figuring the harsher, realer world of adulthood.

For me, that harsher reality has been marked by a tragedy, which is my daughter Rachel's brain injury. Rachel's story appears in these poems (as it does everywhere in my writing) since it is Rachel who sounds the emotional depth charge in my life.

I wrote these in a little notebook first, which is not my usual way of writing poems (I usually compose on the computer). The line lengths were determined by my scrawl and the size of the notebook. When I transposed them onto the computer screen, they looked just right to me. I'm especially proud of the look of these poems—a little messy but also pretty.

The move from lightness to darkness here is also deliberate, though perhaps making for a depressing read. I wanted to parallel the movement from childhood to adulthood and also to get a sense of the conflict of memory and experience, of innocence and wariness.

In general, I like to mix humor with sorrow. Humor for its own sake always strikes me as a little shallow—and tragedy all by itself is hard to get at in a way that feels convincing and unsentimental.

The last thing to mention is that as a fiction writer as well as a poet, my goal is to create work that borrows a little of what I think I do well from each genre. These little pieces, though not narrative poems, are nonetheless like stories that have been crossed by lyric. Lyric stories. In disguise as poems.

Betty Adcock

Place, the Personal, and the Political: Connections

The three poems here are from different decades of my writing life. They have different forms, different subjects, different emotional centers, and different relations to place. Yet as Robert Haas famously said about all the new thinking resembling all the old thinking, let's say that all the new poems resemble all the old poems in being about loss.

An early poem, "Colloquy," appears in none of my books and was lost for a couple of decades. Hovering about this poem are the spirits of the so-called deep imagist poets of the '50s and '60s along with those of the poets, mostly in translation, who influenced them. Its title is ironic since the term means "a conversation," and this poem is about no answer, *no* conversation. Or is it?

In this four-stanza lyric, stanza two is half the length of the eight-line first stanza, and stanza four is half the length of the six-line third. This faint pattern may tell something about the impossibility of any answer in that it shrinks the meditation. Or it could imply that the speaker ceases to have need for answers. The free-verse lines are of varying lengths, dominated by images and repetition of nonspecific questions put to a non-place-specific Nature. Was I thinking all this when I wrote it? No. I was in that place in my head where poems happen, and I play by ear. Later I revised the poem many times, as I do all my poems, yet until I began this essay I had not noticed the pattern of halved stanza lengths. Some things are gifts.

We know nothing about the speaker. An unmetered but discernible rhythm and careful line breaks, engineered during revisions, matter in such a poem. The three-line last stanza, with stress patterns of four, three, and two respectively, acts to further tamp down the intensity the question engendered. The line break between the penultimate and the last line is crucial. An admittedly overbardic final statement offers a different intensity. "It takes us" can mean that it takes our whole lives but also, because of the line break, "it"—meaning the long learning to love a world that refuses us the answers we want to hear—takes us out of ourselves, it takes us over, and it takes us not only toward life but finally toward death as well. Our choice is love or despair.

The second poem, "Penumbra," is very personal and very place specific. No generalizations or broad pronouncements here. The live oak tree with its rope swing was as real as the cracked snapshot of me in 1944 that sits now on my desk. The rooster's name was Chicken Little.

I haven't written or spoken about this poem before, probably because of the intensity of my feelings about the events described. Granted, we do not care much about the facts when reading or writing a poem, yet I often write out of real happenings that I believe can enlarge, warn, embrace, praise, or encompass more than the event itself, with the poet's aggregate experience as lens and the language of poetry as fixative. Please do not report me to the post-postmodernist police.

The place is the back yard of the rambling nineteenth-century house where I lived with my parents until my mother's sudden death from a botched blood transfusion, one month after my sixth birthday. An only child, I had wandered among the orchards and acres and animals of this farm, this "homeplace." My mother's death was an eclipse, a vanishing of light, and it took the life I knew—house, landscape, animals, mother, and my father as I had known him. Everything became strange after we moved to live with my aunt in a small house "in town." I tried to write this poem for years after coming across the snapshot. Only after many rewritings did I discover its present form.

It's been said that the three-line stanza, especially in terza rima, is unstable, that is, that lines reach across stanza breaks in anticipation of the next rhyme, while providing a containing "envelope" rhyme that contradicts the forward motion. This poem is not in terza rima, but that form haunts it; the motion of that form haunts its three-line stanzas, though the rhyme is a x a. Stanzas three, five, and eight are triplets, with their three lines rhyming consecutively and lending emphasis to the information in those stanzas that is important to the poem.

That child in the swing is a figure in a story someone else is telling. The third person distances the reader despite the sadness, at least until the last stanza, when everything changes. As the form changes, the tone changes: stanza length is suddenly four lines instead of three, a quatrain slant-rhyming a b a b; the lines are shortened; third person suddenly becomes *I*. The time becomes now as well as then, the adult voicing what the child knew—somewhat as in stanza eight when time becomes confused with a sudden overlay of vivid colors the child would have seen onto the black-and-white snapshot in the present tense. This is a poem about loss. It is also about the world that cannot answer.

The longer "Fallen" is a very different kind of poem. I call it a lyric narrative and perhaps something of a sermon. The central event is the crash of the space shuttle *Columbia*, which came apart over my home county. Another town had pieces of the spacecraft in the streets, but in my county the bodies fell. This was understandably not reported in the media. My information came from local sources and photographs seen by only a few people. Friends who live there told of the sound, of the piece of hull in a tree, all that I write about. The little Baptist church in the woods was highlighted in my hometown newspaper, the church women feeding the federal searchers.

Not long after the shuttle crash, I read that most of the valuable science is fathered by unmanned spacecraft, that humans are sent up for what amounts to PR for NASA, to keep taxpayers interested in costly space ventures. I thought of a long-ago PBS documentary on space narrated by Carl Sagan. The music that accompanied Dr. Sagan's homage to space exploration, ideas of other life forms, and predicted human colonization of other planets was the music one hears in cathedrals. Hugely expensive space ventures were presented, at least subliminally, as holy.

All this went into the making of "Fallen." The earth does not answer except with itself. The child in the swing is here, furious now at profit and technology-driven political forces that have led to wars, extinctions, vanishing water, poisoned air, dying oceans, and suffering millions in our willed ruin and loss of this "homeplace" that is the only planet to which we'll ever belong. Harsh and risky to write, this poem didn't begin as a political poem. Perhaps it became one.

COLLOQUY

I asked the creatures of grass and air,
the web-weavers and jumpers. I inquired
of crooked sticks and pebbles worn smooth
in the long hyperbole of water.
I asked the trees first, and then their wreaths of birds;
queried mouse, cougar, possum, deer.
I questioned even the deep halls where a congress
of roots holds April a political prisoner.

But there was no word in earth's house.
Branches held sky in their skeletal grasp
without story of prophecy, and the stone
was a deaf mirror.

To love the world is to take into your arms
no answer. It is to give your children
to silence, to the beautiful instructions of millennia
uttered once only, then ringing
far and clear and perfectly
inaudible as the stars.

To love the world that cannot answer
takes losing. It takes us
all our lives.

PENUMBRA

The child in the cracked photograph sits still
in the rope swing hung from a live oak.
Her velvet dress brims with a lace frill.

Her pet Bantam is quiet in her lap.
It is the autumn day of a funeral
And someone has thought to take a snap-

shot of the child who won't be allowed
to go to the burying—the coffin in the house
for days, strange people going in and out.

She's dressed as if she'd go, in the blue church-
dress from last Christmas, almost too short.
The rooster loves her, she guards his perch

on her lap, his colors feathering the mild air.
She concentrates on this, now that her father
is unknowable, crying in his rocking chair.

Her mouth knife-thin, her small hands knotted hard
on the ropes she grips as if to be rescued.
She's growing a will that won't be shed

And something as cold as winter's breath
tightens in her, as later the asthma's vise
will tighten—hands on the throat, the truth.

Black and white, she is hiding
in every one of my bright beginnings.
Gold and deep blue and dark-shining

red the cockerel's feathers, gold the sun
in that skyblue southern fall, blue
over the four o'clocks and the drone

of weeping that drains like a shadow from the house
where someone is gone, is gone, is gone—
where the child will stay to darken like a bruise.

I am six years old, buried
in the colorless album.
My mother is dead.
I forgive no one.

FALLEN

The space shuttle Columbia broke up over several East Texas counties,
including sparsely populated San Augustine County, on the morning of
February 1, 2003.

Silver the winter morning, silver
the early sun downpouring
onto columns of pine and oak, miles
of birdsong-piercing silence silver
in the hour just before the rain;
and our shining myth oncoming, loosening
piecemeal overhead a ghastly charivari

in the high branches, mayhem broken
from the seared-off caul of cold space.

Imagine the torn, deer-haunted woods
where a severed foot still in its boot
was driven into mud. Imagine rags of flesh,
the heart found near a logging road,
the arm in underbrush, insignia beside
an upended helmet filling with icy rain.

Buzzards led the searchers—
                              don't recoil—do
not imagine this a story to be tamed by naming
heroes who died for country and some further bourne
worth dying for.
                   Don't imagine this as anything
beyond the old arc snapped, covenant entirely
broken, our ships no more than silver needles
trying the boundless haystacks of the stars.

Those shadow-stories people lived within
(when we were only hurt and poorly wise)
have hardened into nightmare: heaven
as fleshly destination, hell a fire
we make on earth where myth and science
change partners in the dance.

Only thin February light could plumb the deep
East Texas forests, men combing miles of underbrush
for the whole bloody puzzle, every shard
of failed metal and all the flesh it failed.
Among enormous trees, on a red clay road,
Chinquapin Baptist Church—chosen
beyond all prophecy and imagining—became
receiving station for the shattered dead.

Of course exhausted searchers didn't exhaust
that arboreous dark, its snarled thickets,
its hawk-sharpened air.

Light-footed foxes live there,
wildcats, the invisible cougar, wild boar
winter-thin and hungry, and shuffling armadillos
better armored than the astronauts sent out
as latter knights to press
our argument with airlessness
and make a grail of the mirage our image is,
among the novas and the planetary shrugs.

Disarticulate as temples seized by jungle,
this journey too will disappear. For a while
a mangled piece of the spaceship's hull
swung high in a shagbark hickory,
bell calling what faithful
to the altar of the owl?

Rick Barot

Lucky's Speech

Just about midway through *Waiting for Godot*, one of the most remarkable moments in the play occurs: Lucky speaks. Before this moment of speech, Lucky has been utterly without speech. He is the long-suffering, much-abused lackey of Pozzo, who finds a sadistic glee in making Lucky do everything he wants, no matter how absurd or pathetic: "Stop! (Lucky stops.) Back! (Lucky moves back.) Stop! (Lucky stops.) Turn! (Lucky turns towards auditorium.) Think!"

Given the command to think, what Lucky enacts is a torrent of speaking that lasts over five minutes. These first moments alone will give a sense of that torrent, its mixture of gibberish and portent: "Given the existence as uttered forth in the public works of Puncher and Wattmann of a personal God quaquaquaqua with white beard quaquaquaqua outside time without extension." And on and on.

The moment of Lucky's speech is as disturbing as it moving. In a play that had been choreographing a kind of breezy philosophical banter among its main characters, Lucky's speech and its roaring nonsense is a reminder of the chaos that, like some frequency just beneath our hearing, is always trying to assert itself. The speech also says something about the plaintive recourse that Lucky takes when he is ordered to think: he speaks. Which is to say, speaking is thinking.

Poetry as a barely concealed force in the self. Poetry as pressurized speech. Poetry as near-madness. Poetry as the release point for the world's madness.

For a few years now, Lucky's speech has haunted me. It has also, of course, haunted the poems I've tried to write. This haunting has expressed itself most sharply in the way I've composed my poems, a composition process that has been defined by a longing to arrive at a fuguelike musicality. Repetitive elements of all kinds, periodic sentences that loop and loop, fragments, sly rhymes and ugly rhymes, the grit or soft of particular words—these are the things that I have wanted in my poems.

For years, what I cared about were images. If the images were exact and memorable in any poem I wrote, they were the measure of that poem's success. The visual had a wonderful tyranny. I see now that that love of images was also the love for the quietude that poems can manifest: given a powerful image, the eye can look, the eye can rest.

But to love the music in a poem is to love its motion, the motion that is after all the main imperative of time and the earth. Lucky's speech, as illegible as it is as sense, is nonetheless marvelous as music, rapid and compelling. His speech has patterns, like music, and it is abstract, like music. It is loud, and it is also near. What I have wanted in my recent poems have been those qualities—the brazen, grasping surge after Pozzo's command: "Think!"

THE POEM IS A LETTER OPENER

and it is the letter that is answered
or not answered, held first by the uncle
who sorted it on his graveyard shift
in the postal service warehouse,
after which it became the postman
going from box to box, each box
a particular face like a dog's, the dog
that is also a poem, its eyes dark
like the water in a well, its fur smelling
like grass that is also a poem, green
and exclamatory in spring, later
turning the color of rubber-bands,
which are also poems, holding
together the pencils, the tip-money,
the small stone in the sling-shot right
before it takes flight, the stone that
looks like a tiny skull, granite like death,
a piece of the night left in the middle
of the day, which is also a poem,
starting with its whisper campaign
of morning light, the light touching
the clean sidewalk, the light touching
the sign in the window that says
"No Crying Allowed In This Shop,"
the sign itself a poem, like the dusk

that comes like a cowl around us,
to the sick uncle, to the thieving uncle,
to the uncle who sleeps in the day,
his sleep careful as a tea ceremony
or a poem, a poem that is old and full
of days, a poem like an old china
plate that is the color of time, the dusk
having its supper of fog and people
walking through the fog, the fallen
leaves in the parks like strewn credit
cards, which are also poems, like
the typewriter writing the letter
one little tooth at a time, one love at
a time, in our city of paper and crows.

AFTER DARWISH

I want from love only the beginning.
Not this hillside above the twilight-awakening
city, where you are more absent
for being so present in my mind, the far
cathedral a gold nipple, the surrounding buildings
like silver and black boxes punctured
by their lights pushing out.
                                    I want from love
only the beginning. Not the seaside
where we spoke away the night, the ocean only
an indigo sound, its edges appearing
in melting white lines, while the fog stood
away from us, out where boats swayed
like drunk holiday lights, the air weirdly still
and warm.
                    I want from love only
the beginning. Not the promenade and its rain
at 3AM, the blooms of two umbrellas
and our argument beneath them, as far apart
as the two boroughs separated
by a river, so that even the stone arc

of the bridge couldn't suture the arm's length
we stood from each other.
                              I want from love
only the beginning. Not the confession
you made on another hill: another man, another
figure mobilized out of my dreamscape
terror, the coat rack turning into a man
with antlers, the ficus turning into a man
with green skin. Below us, the city indifferent
with its diamond streets.
                              I want from love only
the beginning. The beginning of one more
conversation in a car, the beginning
of a snow that leaves the day as white
as a hospital, the beginning of an industrial dusk,
the beginning of a new rain, rain that is
the water of the Arno, the water of the Hudson,
the water of the Mississippi, the water of the Nile.

INVENTORY

Bridges and streets. The neon like candy.
Brake lights blooming in rain. Rain.
Concrete. Long live the concrete of cities.

Spoon. Chair. Bed, bread, and stitch.
This language of the house. Blond
light across the mirror. Soap. Salt shaker.

The ginger of you. The cream of you.
The eyes and bones. The scratch-and-sniff
of you. The back. The back of the hand.

Crickets and prairie. The trees standing
like husbands. The gold grass moving,
the pelt of earth. The fence-posts like souls.

Lunch at midnight, dinner at breakfast,
graveyard and swing. Machine that
is the father's pet. Machine that is days.

Breath, reed. Vowels, syllables. Strings.
The bluesman saying, I don't practice,
I throw some meat into the guitar case.

Moon that is the sun of statues. Cornice
pigeons, accordion storefront gates, trash
swirled into cowlick shapes. Box sleepers.

The wish, biding inside like a hive of bees.
The crow, a knuckle of the landscape.
The stone, which is tired of the discursive.

ELECTION SONG

I want to be the governor of Alaska. Because the season
is turning, because the trees are becoming an announcement,
their leaves with the future already in them, the self-arson
of the scarlet leaves, the yellow leaves like superlative
lemons, I want to be the governor of Alaska. Because
I'm tired of the news, the newspapers, the public radio
experts, and my own sad inability to sit quietly in my room,
which Pascal declares is the problem with people, I want
to be the governor of Alaska. Because from the air base
and army base outside my town, airplanes as gray as whales
and as big as dreams keep flying over our houses,
shrieking like oversized skateboards on city sidewalks.
Because of arsenic in the rain, because of arsenic sleeping
inside the ground, and the weather like a cold war always
coming down from Canada and Russia, I want to be
the governor of Alaska. Because I'm always hearing speech
from the kettles and the door-knobs, those pure products
of America, their soft words always scurrying, things

bothered by eyes and light. Because I have been reading
the letters of van Gogh, the part where he says, "Instead of
painting the ordinary wall of the mean room, I paint
infinity." Because when he died the world went dark by half,
and when you went away this morning the other half went
dark, I want to be the governor of Alaska. Because of all
the Filipinos canning tuna in Alaska, because of the
mail-order brides ordered by the lonely men of Alaska,
I want to be the governor of Alaska. Because of the pipeline
on the state's chest like a bypass scar, because of the streams
and flowers of the tundra, alive so briefly they are
like the gift of an election blossoming every four years,
I want to be the governor of Alaska. Because of the price
of gas, because of the rosaries I prayed in my childhood,
I want to be the governor of Alaska. Because even then,
in childhood, I knew it was doubt that made people small,
when I was dared to eat a caterpillar, I did. It wasn't shooting
moose, but still it made me want to be the governor of Alaska.

WRIGHT PARK

There must be drugs in the backpack.
One cop is leading away the bicycle,
while the other cops stand around the man
handcuffed on the ground, not moving
but clearly not hurt, waiting like everyone else
for what will happen next.
It's just one faggot on a bicycle,
says the old man standing near me,
why so many cops?
                            The park is beautiful
at dusk. The sky a blue-gray dome.
The lawns like billiard tables. The hundred
trees exhaling a good, cold air.
The statue of Ibsen looks over
the pond's mallards, the dog-walkers
and the smoking teenagers, the men beginning
to gather among the trees.

I don't know about violence, but what I see
is an old man in a blue ski jacket
on a summer evening, his cane thin and white
as a toothpick,
                not stick enough
to beat back the faggots riding into the park
on their bicycles, the faggots in the flower beds,
the faggots that are the blue cops,
the faggots in the trees and bushes,
the faggots splashing into the pond of ducks
and carp, the faggots on the swings,
the faggots, the faggots everywhere, the faggots.

Debra Allbery

The Grace of Accuracy

AFTER VERMEER

1. Woman Holding a Balance

Still the map surprises. What's near now,
what's newly distant. Nothing finds me here,
no letters, none of my usual dreams.
Overcast warps through the leaded glass
of our bedroom window, the morning light
presses into a porcelain cup on the sill.

My husband's eyes move beneath his lids
as if he were reading. Last night I dreamed him
standing on a ladder in the rain,
trying to clear out some leaf-clogged gutters,
while below his father muttered advice to the ground,
hand raised in an irritated benediction.
Then my husband lifted a small doll by one heel
from the eaves, brackish water draining
from its joints, its open eyes.

Is it ever how we've imagined? I wake up lost,
then watch the dawn's dim shadows take on weight,
and the room becomes every other room
where I have lived, the window any window
I've looked through. Outside, the threadbare browns
of early winter, the frost-stunned grass,

tiny tremors of wind. The inanimate
take on life for a moment, then are revealed:
a scrap of writing paper, a discarded glove.
Sympathy—the word hung in a glass charm
from a gold bracelet I wore when I was a girl.

What is mine now is only what I keep to myself—
a clutch of secrets like the tightened mass
of another life inside me, a phantom fullness
I can never name, a quickening.
And yet in marriage what isn't given away?
Without looking back, I can see his sleep,
the way the worn light finds him, darkness
folding itself away like a heavy drape.
And in his dream, perhaps, is my own hand,
resting on the clean edge of a table.

2. Girl Asleep at a Table

The inside-out of waking, my blue-lipped dream
just breaking up: a banquet, your late entrance.
The guests' eyes lifting,
turning a question toward me.

I saw your shadow leaning in the doorway.
You bowed to me with an absurd flourish.
Something wrong with your smile,
the shape of your teeth.

This morning in Greyfriars churchyard
an old man limped toward me, apologizing
for his outstretched hand.
See my head keeps bleeding, he said,

and my hands. My hands are broke.
He turned them over and over
as if in wonder, his wet-dog smell
roping itself around me, and I backed away—

not frightened of him, just angry
at my own wants. I mumbled sorry
and hurried out the gates. His scent
ghosting around me, rising from the cobbles.

I lost myself in the market,
all the damp vendors and their cold flowers.
A blind man took my wrist—*You're happy today*—
and I couldn't answer, held by his unfixed stare.

Home now, by this fire, I can't get warm.
Still, it's enough to be inside, to just sit still
here at this table and lean my head
against my hand, feel how it feels to lean,

to rest against something. As sleep hovers,
touches, enters. Always, always, it murmurs,
a breath from your grave. You used to palm
the word, play shell games with it.

Now, love, it's no mystery. Close your eyes.
The room is the same inside me, then falls away.
Crosshatch, spindle. Just blind lost light.
Only my own hands holding me up.

3. Woman in Blue Reading a Letter

The calm passes overhead like cloud shadow,
darkens the eggshell walls.

Outside, spring's rainlight,
the pale new medallions of leaves

caught in the wind's strumming.
The closer I come to my confinement,

the more I shawl my past around me.
Three months now he's sailed. I pull

old boxes down, finger trinkets from my childhood—
a tiny pin shaped like a beetle, a twig

in a sealed jar once filled with river water.
Its green still dusts the glass.

And in a box of letters, one stamped
and addressed to my grandmother, labeled

To be opened when I am grown up.
How strange to deliver this to myself

twenty-five years later—how strange
to me, my own young hand. The letters

curled back into themselves,
small fists, ferns still furled.

I write of a flood. Simple descriptions:
The streets are like rivers. Our water isn't safe.

I can't remember why I chose to save this.
I remember the flood. Seeing my father out in it.

And the smell—the waterlogged bricks
in our cellar, crumbling to the touch.

Sometimes I dream our child is buried alive.
I know where she is, but still I choose to ignore her

and she's furious, down in her little pocket of earth,
angry enough to claw her own escape.

Who would I tell this to. If I stand still enough
the room's silence and mine create a sound

between them, the round note
of a cello, a generated third.

HOW TO EXPLAIN PICTURES TO A DEAD HARE

Joseph Beuys at Galerie Schmela
Dusseldorf, 1965

1.
The woman walks a bramble
of quiet fright, her tenses
frayed. Any pencil touch
not light enough.

No Leda. Only fierce
ur-flight, a thrum, a wish of wings—
Only dashed speech, then
upsweep, the god's ascent.

How the hand knows
its own name and writes it
blind. Then something washes
over the word.

Golgotha. Or else Kleve,
after the war. A dream I had once—
ochre shouts, a *braunkreuz*
thrown through the thick breath of shadows.

2.
True is this event during the war:
When the Tartars found me after the planecrash
they wrapped me in felt and fur,
they salved my wounds with lard.

Sometimes these things are looked at
in a false way, these accidents, damages
to my body, these wounds. They are not secret
affinities. They are not only mine.

3.
Gold leaf pressed into
his face's harrowed gaunt.
Soft slack of the animal
in his arms, his stroke piano—

4.
This is a map of the ruined city,
a shaft of lightning in the pine.
Blood sky, foxed twilight,
the trees sound like waiting.

This is a word thought
but not spoken. This is how
it listens to itself—its slow whorl
of force, the sure press of its thumbprint.

The Grace of Accuracy

> The painter's eye follows relation out.
> His work is not to paint the visible,
> He says, it is to render visible.
> —Howard Nemerov

> The painter's vision is not a lens,
> It trembles to caress the light.
> —Robert Lowell

Ut pictura poesis: As in painting, so in poetry. Like the painter in the passages above, the poet—in writing about the visual arts (or, for that matter, writing in response to a memory, landscape, object, emotion, another poem)—aims not to merely describe but to *render*: to take in and draw forth, to translate and transform—in order to see into, see further, to answer vision with vision. Ekphrasis—the verbal representation of the visual arts—may take its cue from the art's subject matter or its style of composition, but the impulse is both parallel and participatory. "The poet, like the painter, is both rescuer and recon-structor," says Charles Wright. And Nemerov: "Both poet and painter want to reach the silence behind the language, the silence within the language." From the Greek, *ekphrasein*: "to speak in full."

That effort to reach the silences behind and within language was the impetus for my sequence of poems entitled "After Vermeer." They came about through a kind of immersion in the *tone* of Vermeer's interior spaces, their representa-tions of the private mind, of contemplation that believes itself unobserved; they rose out of an effort (borrowing a phrase from Tomas Tranströmer's wonderful poem "Vermeer") *to go through walls*. I'm drawn to the idea of a painting as an iconostasis—as a screen, portal, passageway, as a point of departure— for the poem. These poems aren't intended to "narrate" the paintings named in the sec-tion titles or to give voice to the particular women depicted in them. The aim, rather, was to enter and inhabit the reverberations of those still spaces—their vibrant and precise balances between interior and exterior, the seen and the un-seen, "the world about us and the world within us" (Stevens)—and listen. That radiographs have shown that the "Woman Holding a Balance" is *not* weighing gold or pearls (as was once believed) but is testing an empty scale, that there originally was a man in the doorway behind the "Girl Asleep at a Table" (Ver-meer later painted him out)—these facts only made the paintings more hospi-table for the meditations they occasioned on marriage, on motherhood, on the very notion of privacy that Vermeer conveys with such brilliance.

I began thinking about "How to Explain Pictures to a Dead Hare" after attending a Joseph Beuys retrospective. I felt a great affinity for his methods and mythic resonances—his obsessive use of mutable materials and totemic symbols, his elemental Lascaux-like palette. I was particularly drawn toward his watercolors and accounts and photographs of his *actionen* ("actions"), his term for performance art. The action that the poem title identifies provided a context; it was ekphrastic in its very nature, but at the same time it challenged the presumptions inherent in "explaining" art.

There are photographs and eyewitness accounts of this 1965 gallery event: Beuys, his face covered with honey and gold leaf, carried a dead hare from draw-ing to drawing (these were his own works), stroking the animal and talking to it quietly—too quietly for those observing to hear.

So, in this case the artwork and the artist provided the compositional struc-ture and method for the poem, as well as, in one section, the speaker. Each of the quatrains in the first section is my own rapid sketch of a Beuys pencil drawing or watercolor—simple, impressionistic lines. I wrote these very quickly and made few revisions. The second section takes on the persona of the artist himself, providing biographical and aesthetic context. The third section shifts in point of view; the final section returns to the "explanations."

Whether or not the materials of his art—felt, fur, lard— were the ones that saved his life after the 1944 plane crash (he later denied his own account), the effort to get to the essential and archetypal through art was what drew me to these works. In my recasting of comments he made in a 1980 interview: "They are not private affinities; they are not only mine."

Ekphrasis being, at the heart of things, concerned with composition, an ekphrastic poem often functions, too, as an ars poetica. In looking into a painting, we're seeking instruction, guidance; we study how another artist "follows relation out." In the early years of my apprenticeship, Lowell's ars poetica "Epilogue" provided the text for my matins and my vespers; it remains a touchstone, a credo. *The painter's vision is not a lens*, Lowell says, but rather a recognition (rescue, reconstruction) of what Stevens called "the universal poetry reflected in everything" and, as such, an effort to honor what passes and what endures:

> Pray for the grace of accuracy
> Vermeer gave to the sun's illumination
> stealing like the tide across a map
> to his girl solid with yearning.

Thomas Lux

How Far Out It Goes

It has always been difficult to talk about what the process of writing a poem is like for me, other than that every poem takes many drafts and that I try to follow Mr. Frost's dictum "No surprise for the writer, no surprise for the reader." I also favor stamina and doggedness. I'll try to do a little more here by writing about these two poems because my colleagues at the MFA Program for Writers at Warren Wilson asked me to. I was on the faculty for well over twenty years, and I am deeply indebted to the program and to the dozens of other poets and fiction writers there, faculty and students, who taught me so much.

THE PIER ASPIRING

See if you can see how far out it goes. See? You can't see the end!
I'd take you out there
but it's a six-hour walk
and the work's redundant: one board laid down after another.
When the sun is high
the boards are hot.
Splinters always pose a problem walking any other way but straight.
What keeps me working on it, driving piles,
hauling timber, what's kept my hand
on the hammer, the barnacle scraper,
what keeps me working through the thirst,
the nights when the waves' tops pound
the pier from beneath, what keeps me glad
for the work, the theory is, despite the ridicule
at the lumberyard, the treks with pails
of nails (my arms

two centimeters longer each trip), the theory
is this: it's my body's habit,
hand over foot, paycheck to paycheck,
it's in the grain of my bones,
lunch bucket to lunch box.
It's good to wear an X
on my back, to bend my back to the sky, it's right
to use the hammer and the saw,
it's good to sleep
out there—attached at one distant end
and tomorrow adding to that distance.
The theory
is: It will be a bridge.

I don't think the subject of an ars poetica, i.e., an attempt to describe the nature of poetry, was listed among suggested topics/angles we use to speak about our poems, but I'd like to try with this poem. The title evolved from something I found in quotes in my notebook: someone referred to a pier as a disappointed bridge. I was struck by the image. My poems often begin with a title, a few words that *suggest* something. I like to think of poems as bridges, a fundamental and not overly original metaphor for one thing that connects to another thing, often over perilous heights and across scary waters. At one end of the bridge is the writer, at the other end the reader. It's a persona poem as well as an ars poetica. Persona *was* one of the topics/angles for this anthology. Two for one! The guy who is building the pier is on the land end of it talking to someone and telling him/her about the pier. He's a little bit agitated. The speakers of my poems are often agitated. The poem uses hyperbole (a fun tool in our toolbox) and understatement (not as much fun but necessary lest the hyperbole become merely hyperbole). I'm trying to wring a little irony out of the "splinters" line: it's not always best to avoid splinters by walking straight only. The line is also deliberately all trochaic, to give the effect of tumbling forward. He (the speaker) is trying to figure out why he keeps building (writing) his pier even though it includes manual labor (let's face facts: poetry, writing, is work), isolation (some nights he sleeps out on the pier to save a total twelve-hour round-trip walk to and from work!), and ridicule when he keeps buying more boards at the lumberyard. He even suffers a certain level of bodily harm: elongated arms! Do you, citizen reader, have any idea what a pail of nails weighs? Serious elbow problems could result, I was told by an orthopedist. He doesn't make any grand statements about the enormity of his task; he doesn't babble about the spheres; he likes the work, which does not include a quill pen or a doily. He might slip into a moment of self-pity when he refers to a target on his back, but the only things aimed at that target are the sun, the sky, time—and we all wear those targets on our backs. His goals are modest: he wants his pier to connect, to communicate, with an other (deliberately two words), who would be the reader. As the more and more moribund theorists would have us believe (and they are partly right): language is indeterminate; therefore it is not to be trusted. Imperfect as it may be, it is still the best thing we have, the best chance we have, of truly communicating with each other. The theorists may sulk and bitch, but they haven't come up with anything better.

THE SHOOTING ZOO

The giraffe can't stand up anymore: he's still tall
but not tall enough. The silverback is bald,
the zebra's black stripes gray. There's a virus at the zoo: the spring-
bok can't prong,
the alligators wracked by cataracts,
the last lion meowls like an auntie's cat.
The penguins walk as if they have a load in their pants!
The vultures are eating sandwiches and plants!
Something's wrong with all the animals: the pandas obstreperous,
the iguanas demand bananas, the loons
are out of tune.
What to do, what to do? Soon,
whatever it is deranging them
will pass through their bars,
across their moats,
and then: our dogs and gold-
fish, the little parakeet
who pecks our lips
so we may say it kisses us, soon
they'll start dropping too.
Next: our children, grandma?
The zookeepers don't know what to do, so
print some permits permitting men
to bring their guns to the shooting zoo.

I don't remember exactly how this poem started. I don't think the title came from a notebook or my reading. Maybe it just occurred to me. These two words together constitute a kind of oxymoron. And: they repeat, very close together, one of the softest and most suggestive vowel sounds in our language: *oo*. If you pass up an opportunity to at least explore the possibilities put forth, well, then you would be required to return your poetic license and expect no refund! I think I knew right away—I got the signal from the title—that I wanted to really load up the sonics in this poem, I wanted to have lots of sound play (rhyme), internally as well as end rhymes. Something's wrong with the animals. It's not a sob-sister anti-zoo poem: I think the problem, the poem's *argument*, has more to do with the human tendency, when we don't understand or when we fear something, our first reaction is: let's kill the motherfucker! We need to see that thing as a threat to ourselves, our children, even our senior citizens, so that we can justify a violent reaction to it. I think that's a kind of moral point I'm trying to make with all the crazy stuff that's going on with the animals. They're not acting normal. I'm trying to lull the reader a bit in the first half of the poem, and then I try to slip in a little dark nugget or two, as warning signs, before the guys with the guns show up.

Stuart Dischell

The Song Can Also Be a Story

EVENING IN THE WINDOW, PARTS I–IV

i

She and he sit in the open window and if you saw them
You would say that most everything is white around them—
The painted walls, the high ceiling, the open curtain
Whose blue and green flowers are pressed between the folded
Pleats, and most of all the white stone buildings like the one
Across the narrow street where things have always happened.
It is a double window in the French style but of modern
Design. One floor up from the pavement, she and he
Drink and smoke: he keeping his weight on his feet as he leans
On the sill; she perching, her back against the right
Frame; both taking their places each evening though
Neither needs to say it, as in the way they silently chose
Who made the first touch, what side of the new bed
To take as their own. And if you saw them that evening
In the window just as it was closing when the white
Of the sky matched the white of the stone and the white
Curtain through the light revealed its bright pattern in
The moment after their fingers hinged and released, you would
Think they were not parting but removing what was left between them.

ii

He walked past the window and if you were watching you
Would know they were no longer there since that evening, their last

96

Together when they drank and smoked and talked about themselves
And watched the narrow street that was their street for a time
When they still could talk about what they had left between them.
The glass was black as the street and the sky as absent of light
As the room behind the drawn curtains in their frames where
He pictured the twin beds they had pushed together, her clothes
Scattered to be packed, and the last image of their bodies glazed
In the mirror, when she had said, "Look." It was no longer their season
She told him later, as if she were speaking of the pitted fruit of summer—
But true enough the heat of the city was gone and the stone buildings
That had absorbed it were cold in the dark. He never had been in this
City in winter before, never had felt the wind this way off the river
Through the elevated and narrow streets, could not keep from coming
    back
To the one that passed beneath their window where they had leaned
    together—
Where they had drank and smoked and talked in summer and closed
The window and took off their clothes and parted the next morning
At the station near the ruins. Had you seen him again you would know
    them.

iii
She stood alone in the window of a fine hotel room
In the city she last saw when he was the same age she had
Become. His spirit filled the empty place beside her on the sill
Just as she knew this would happen when she returned
To this city where she and he once stood in the window
Of the apartment they had rented in a nearby quarter
Where they drank and smoked and talked about everything
But their future. She was twice as old now as she was that summer.
Jet-lagged a little, lying in bed after dinner, she had forgotten
How long it stayed light out. She pictured their last evening
In the window together, how it was they were with each other,
The bedspread and top sheet pushed to either side of them
Like curtains, the plaster ceiling like the wall of the building
Across the street from the apartment they had taken
Near the ruins where they did not have to be secret
(You might have seen them), where they closed the window

That last evening together, a black and white series she would paint later
Across the threads of a canvas: a man's arms around the blurred figure
Of a woman in motion at the edge of the bed to what waited beyond them.

iv
The years gone by did not treat the city well and the age
It slipped into was like those it had endured in the past.
Its government fell; public buildings were set on fire
Once more by its own citizens. Occupying armies
Awaited treaties inside the former gates. The black soot
Cleaned from the structures a century before built up again,
And the walls of the building across the street from the window
Where he and she talked and smoked in the evening
That summer had long darkened into shadow. You might say
The weather had altered with the city's fortunes.
The river froze in winter and colonies of rats grew fearless.
There were sieges and shortages and power failures.
Graves were looted and zoo animals slaughtered.
The frame where she and he once sat and talked in the window
And drank and smoked was now sealed with bricks the last
Residents loosened from the pavement and with stones quarried
From the ruins. The quarter was empty but not as it was
The August of their inhabitation when others were merely traveling.
Whoever you are, whatever you saw, what is it you still ask from them?

To talk about the way a poem was written begs a discussion that concerns the degree of consciousness a writer has regarding the writing process, as well as the literal and temperamental climates present during composition and revision. As for me, I have rarely begun a poem thinking it would be of the structural or formal design it would ultimately become. Usually at some early point in my writing, I follow a potential that lies within the newly created language and lineation—even when the strategy aspires to artlessness. It is easier later on to think back say, "look what I have done."

I wrote and revised the poems that comprise "Evening in the Window, Parts I–IV" over the course of about a year. I wrote them separately though sequentially and with not a thought till far along that they would be arranged as sections of a quartet. When I wrote the initial poem, I entitled it "Them," which is also the final word of the poem and the sections that follow. My interest in it lasted but a few hours when I recalled "Them" was also the title of a 1950s horror film. I retitled the draft "Evening in the Window" and did not know then that I would use its single stanza, long-lined structure as a pattern.

In certain of the poems in my previous book, *Backwards Days*, it had been helpful for me to cool hot thoughts through craft, especially by the use of stanzas, to give a sense of organization to the mess of my emotions. Similarly, years later, in the poems that would comprise "Evening in the Window, Parts I–IV," I created a structure that might contain in its rhythms the stages of heartbreak—from mania to despondency. I guess I opted for the single stanza—in this case nineteen lines—as a large room to hold the rush of obsessive rhetoric and syntax engaged in the repetition of individual words and phrasings as I had tried to build cadence out of them. I wanted the lines to go as far as they could without touching the right-hand margin.

A dear, brilliant poet friend with many ideas about the lyric was put off by what he construed as my use of narrative—but I was already too close to the people in my poem and needed to have an off-the scene narrator rather than a more intimate speaker. I believe in this case, the narrator allowed the poem to be both outside the events of the poem and inside the minds of the participants. Still, I hope the rhythms of the poem are akin to that of the lyric: the story can also be a song.

The window in the poem hangs along the rue Rollin, a one-block street in Paris, a few doors down from where Descartes lived when the street was called rue Neuve St-Etienne after the nearby ancient church of St-Etienne du Mont. Pascal also resided down the block, as did Charles Rollin, the Jansenist theologian, for whom the street eventually was named. Near the Arenas de Lutece and the Place Contrescarpe, it is in one of the oldest civilized parts of Paris, a high street where the Romans preferred to live rather than what people commonly call the Latin Quarter near the river. The rue Rollin is remarkably quiet, off-limits to cars and trucks except for deliveries.

I wrote Part I in Greensboro, North Carolina, in the midcentury modern ramshackle house I live in—set back from the street with ivy-covered lawn and trees. Remarkably, via email the "she" of the poem helped me to revise it. When there was no longer conversation between us, I drafted sections II and III in Paris in a tiny studio in the rue de Savoie, another narrow quiet street. Section IV was also written back in Greensboro. Initially, I thought I might punctuate a manuscript with these poems, but over time it felt best to have them under the one title, "Evening in the Window, Parts I–IV."

Dana Levin

No Elegies

declares the upper right-hand corner, underlined twice and just to the right of a jagged lightning bolt. Midpage, the bolt splits **WORM** from **REFUGE FIELD** in a doodled throng of stars and boxes, a festival of snaking lines, then: *every body // a cocoon of change*—and a command banding the page-bottom: **CUL-TIVATE THIS FIELD OF BLISS.** Four phrases, black as stamps: 9/23/03.

My father and then my mother had died.

~

Emotion finds its root in Latin: *e—motio*, to move out. It's a given that those of us who are called to the poetic art are often following the voice of strong feeling: every poem, at its heart, an involuntary cry the poet has made into song. Listen for the gasps of outrage and ecstasy fueling Ginsberg's *Howl*, the "ill-spirit sob" of Lowell's *Skunk Hour*, even the round-mouthed eurekas at the core of Stevensian cool.

Knicked skin, sudden win, night caress, someone dies: something happens, and it makes you open your mouth. You're struck—you let out a sound.

~

When death has pierced you (first him and then her in the space of six months) and you deny yourself lamentation—when you deny yourself available forms of grief (you, a believer in forms)—when you refuse to memorialize, eulogize, or in any way sing before a tomb—

Forms have feelings. It was the *feelings* offered by traditional elegy I rejected:

"Classical elegies start out with a statement of the subject (usually a specific death), followed by the lamentations or mourning of this death, and finally consolation, as the poet comes to accept the loss," states Padgett's *Handbook of Poetic Forms*. Mourning? It was a private hell, writing about it head-on unendurable. Consolation? It seemed beyond the depths of my death-shock. Acceptance? Well,

there was acceptance and then there was *acceptance*: NO ELEGIES I scored, with a black Staedtler pigment liner. I wanted to look that fucker death in the face.

~

Emotion: a stirring, a moving, an agitation, a perturbation, a migration; so says the OED. I refused to prop my bare grief up on the dais of the page, but still my involuntary cry demanded audience (L. *audientia*, to hear). Circumventing elegy meant finding new forms for the grief-cry, new lenses through which to see the human end. I began to study corpse-decay, the life cycles of diptera; became an adherent of Tibetan Buddhist teachings, which hinge on the fact of our impermanence; meditated on psychedelic images of White Tara, Tibetan mother of compassion and long life; examined photos of sarcophagidae, the pupa of the cheese-skipper "recovered in Egyptian mummies, Mexican tomb shafts, and in the skulls of ancient bison." I began to write poems based on research and dream, taking dictation from the worms and the gods.

"Refuge Field," "The Mentor," and "Augur" are some of the fruits of that first refusal of elegy. "The Mentor" stems, verbatim, from a dream journal entry and preserves that initial prose form. I began to write many prose poems, and short lyrics, and long verse sequences: turning from elegy left me formally restless; in aversion I found invention. Death as muse led to poems like "Refuge Field," where the worms and the gods met at the charnel ground: the "Eight Great Cemeteries" mentioned in the poem were prominent cemeteries of ancient India, important meditation fields for tantric adepts and monks to confront impermanence in the raw. It was, of course, not the charnel grounds of India but my back yard, with its night-crickets and cicadas, its larvae and webs, that became my devotion field.

And "Augur": it was the last to be written and is the first to appear in the book that developed from my grief conversions. Such a placement—the poem of

aftermath opening the book of loss—seems right for a poem called "Augur,"
named for the ancient Roman seer. I consider it a reverse elegy: its long lines
spool out and reel in short, spool out again in a kind of frantic seeking, a seeking
against lament. Four years after my parents died, my sister died: well and then
sick and then dead in three weeks. I was sick of death, and I was sick of grief: I
looked to signs, wondered if I could live, find a new song in my mouth.

REFUGE FIELD

You have installed a voice that can soothe you: *agents
      of the eaten flesh, every body*

      a cocoon of change—

Puparium. The garden
      a birthing house, *sarcophagidae—*

And green was so dark in the night-garden, in the garden's
      gourd of air—

green's epitome
      of green's peace, the beautiful inhuman

leg-music, crickets'
      thrum—
a pulse

      to build their houses by,
each
      successive molt

a tent of skin
      in which skin can grow, the metallic sheen
of their blue backs

      as they hatch out, winged and mouthed—

Like in a charnel ground, you sit and see.

In one of the Eight Great
    Cemeteries, you sit and see—

How the skull-grounds
    are ringed by flame, how they spread out under

a diamond tent, how the adepts
    pupate
among bones—

    saying I who fear dying, I who fear
being dead—

    Refuge field.

    See it now.

That assembly of sages you would have yourself
    build,
to hear the lineage
    from mouth to ear, encounter the truth-

    chain—

saying, *Soft eaters, someone's children, who gives them*
    refuge from want—

Cynomyopsis Cadavarena. On every tongue
    they feed.

THE MENTOR

The Mentor was in town to give a lecture, he was staying in my apartment. Too sick to attend, his wife stayed behind and I to nurse her. That night, the Mentor still away, curled in pain, she crept to my room to sleep with me. Hunched in bed she cried and shook, and in the morning when I woke up she was dead. I cradled her dead body in misery, for now I had to tell the Mentor.

I tracked him to a diner and found him in a booth drinking coffee. He was jovial, began showing me a collection of organa: eggs, sea shells, stones, pond water in jars—I grab his hand mid-flourish, say, "Have you seen your wife?" And he looks confused, something gassing his eyes, he says, "Is she gone?" getting upset, and then smiling, saying, "When she comes back, I don't think she'll come back as a person, I think she'll come back as her clothes—she loved them so, the threads, the dyes—" Then he is staring into a tin can full of water, murky water almost red, and I know this will be our science: mourning her.

AUGUR

Hawk perched low on a hedge of vine.

On hunt for what hid
    in the tangle.

The small citizens, mouse and gopher.

Body of Ra the hawk signified.

In the symbol book, which I opened after climbing the stairs,
    after the hawk fanned out its banded tail like I should

    pick a card—

The book was a prisoner of my ardor for the dark—through it I stalked,
    a seeker.

It was a character out of a Victorian novel—*Symbol Book*, an
    imbecile, a Dutch inventor.

Saying You must bow
    to the Hippogriff (half-raptor, half-horse), it must

    lower its head to your hand.

Halcon Pradeno. Mexicano. Come to me for my winter ground.

According to whatbird.com.

Hawk perched low on a hedge of vine. Going
    heel to toe, so as not to startle.

Cloud unhooding *body of Ra* a pale pearl of winter sun—

Renaissance printers
    often stamped their wares with a hooded falcon,

    emblem of the dungeoned seer.

That "hope for light" the darkened nourish.

Closed books, *post tenebras spero lucem* along the spine—

I found the phrase in the Office for the Dead, in the Latin Vulgate:
    after darkness I hope for light—

Then: *hell is my house, and in darkness I have made my bed*—

I thought of my father and mother and sister being dead, I was so sick
    of feeling anything about it—

The hood stood for hope of liberty.

Of wanting to swoop and soar over enormous swells,
    as in my dream.

I hovered high, I could see the mammals in the raucous waters, their slick
skins
    of danger and wonder.

My soul hath thirsted, the Vulgate said, *He hath put a new song into my
mouth*.

The hawk appeared. Unhooded.
    An auspice, from *auspex, avispex*, "one who looks at birds"—

I'd been wanting to know if it was all right to live.

An ascensional symbol on every level, the symbol book said.

Body of Ra. Solar victory. If one can believe the book
of symbols.

Reginald Gibbons

Greco-Russianizing

MIRROR

> Into the dressing-table mirror a triptych cup of cocoa
>   Disappears, the window-curtain sways and straight out
> The narrow path to the orchard, into toppled trees and chaos,
>   The mirror rushes toward the swings.
>   —Boris Pasternak

A round of thanks or
       Drinks for
My three favorite books—
       Let's stand
Them on their fleet or
       Swollen
Stylistic feet for
       Photos,
Sotto voce they
       Conspire,
With pen-feather arms
       Around
Each other's inky
       Wings—Hey!
You two outer ones,
       Turn in
A little! They hinge
       Themselves
Into a dressing-
       Table

Looking-glass in a
      Hushed house.
(Where is everyone?)

In their tiny choir,
      At worst
They sing song-tricks, and
      The e-
Lixir for which they
      Thirst is
That first cup of hot
      Cocoa
In Pasternak's poem
      That in
His Russian I can't
      Read and
In my English I
      Can't for-
Get. His reflected
      China
Cup and inflected
      Language
Outlive coups, blues, re-
      Volu-
Tions, the tournaments
      Of grave-
Diggers, ornaments
      Of verse,
Anniversaries
      Of words
With bad lives and brok-
      En backs.
My three favorite books!—
      Mirrors
Canted side by side
      To guide
Whatever's looking
      Into

Them—praise their age and
     Pages!
That cup of loco zooms
     Through the
Window out a path
     Among
Glad shadows beneath
     Blue trees,
While into these rooms
     Those same
Trees keep crowding but
     Their bent
Strong limbs touch and break
     Nothing.
The lantern by which
     Something
Was written at this
     Table,
But not yet a chant
     Or kiss:
Is it burning here,
     Hissing,
Or softly searching
     Dear paths,
Hovering out there?

BECAUSE OF APHRODITE

The sweeping force with which
     Anything could be thrown—
A javelin—or the
     Battering blows of hot
Winds, and these gusts, too: rain,
     Desire, wildfire's rushing
Noise, and fast-falling stone-
     Cold night in lands of bone-
Hard darkness and screaming
     Storm blasts that freeze the blood.

But in our stillness, a
      Gnat's wings buzz, plucked lyre strings
Beat slightly out of tune,
      Soft lights on low far shores
Of the bay at sundown
      Are trembling, and then two
Leaping dolphins blow in
      Mid-arc and again dive
Into dark blue, and an
      Eagle wings up from the
Water toward our bluff and
      Past us just overhead,
Heavily climbing air
      With fierce soft pinions, we
Hear three strokes and it's gone,
      And your eyes are pulsing
Out the light of your in-
      Tensity, flashing from
Some rocky point within.

      A strong scent of wood smoke,
Small bellows are blowing
      The iron-melting flames to
A roar, you fan me, fan
      Yourself, then like glowing
Javelins we're both hurled.

Amid the froth of poetic epiphenomena, I still get pleasure from refreshing the contemporary moment, our moment, with the past. The epigraph to "Mirror" is from a poem of the same title by Boris Pasternak, one of the poems he collected in his early book, *My Sister—Life*, which announced his great poetic gifts and dazzled Russian readers. In Russian, *life* is a feminine noun, so the title expresses a kinship with the female, yet because life is a sister, this kinship has nothing to do with romantic love or eros and everything to do with a close, intense bond between poet and experience, poet and world, poet and change, poet and language itself—all sisters. Pasternak's moment was the ominous summer of 1917, when the poet composed this book at the age of twenty-seven. And yet Pasternak is said to have written the whole sequence of fifty poems when he had fallen in love … (again). So the intensity of the way that language itself *perceives* is somehow related to the intensity of romantic love.

What so drew me to the Russian poem, when I (without any Russian) was at work translating it with Ilya Kutik, was the way it moves: veering to the next image or idea because the sounds of words draw it that way. And flinging itself into metaphors and through them in different directions. (In his youth there was a Russian avant-garde group of poets—although it was not his group—called "Centrifuge.") My pleasure is in the movement of this poem, which is "about" a kind of intoxication of impressions, of mood, of place.

I have learned that Russian words have much bigger, more various clouds of connotation around them than do English words. When we read translations of Pasternak (or, to take a similar example, Marina Tsvetaeva), the variety of the English-language versions seems baffling and must have to do with the fact that the English-language mind of the translator has to choose a word that inevitably not only does not match the connotations of the Russian word (a problem for all literary translators) but also itself has a narrower range of connotations than does the Russian word. The higgledy-piggledy translated sequences of images in a poem by Pasternak usually make little poetic sense to us, because we're cut off from the music of the poem, the sound-allusions and sound-links of "the secondary meanings of the words" (T. S. Eliot). Even if our minds are free enough, our English-language ears are unavoidably covered by sound-canceling, and thus meaning-canceling, headphones. We're listening to the poem through a language that for cultural reasons more than linguistic ones has narrowed the original into too constricted, and too circumspect, a dance.

The playfulness of the movement in Pasternak's poem isn't superficial but rather exuberantly serious, and from what I can tell, it arises from what we would consider a mystical stance toward language (something nearly unknown in contemporary American or English poetry and, for good-enough English-language reasons, hard to trust). Our American pragmatism or our mode of self-display or our sense of language rules it out. (I think that we could accept it and use it, if we could see it not as mystical but as simply part of the legacy of the history of poetry—all of which is available to us in our "anthology without walls"—to paraphrase André Malraux on visual art.)

And what if readers don't *want* to follow in their own language such devices as Russian poets have used? I have chosen not to worry about it and instead have written a poem in homage to Pasternak that may fling itself further than it would have gone if I had stuck to what I have been comfortable doing in a poem.

Except that I am never entirely comfortable in that way. I look for the bookcase word that swings open if I push on it just so while touching a particular phoneme. Or, if I look through a word rather than at it, for the window that appears where there was none before. What I now perceive in my "Mirror" is that the poem about books leads to love, and that calls to the following poem, on desire. And in "Because of Aphrodite," which is put together in a different way, I listen for a whole room already filled with the furniture of metaphors, a room that stands, I sense, beyond a windowless wall of my own lines, and I try to find the angle of a word-window that will let me get to it. "Everything is a door—the light pressure of a thought is enough" (Octavio Paz). Meanwhile, everyday relations with others, preoccupations, sorrows, perceptions, angers, thankfulness, keep me on course toward what I turn out to be able, now and then, to imagine and say.

Joan Aleshire

Learning from Time & the Poem Itself

I write, or scrawl, rough, sprawling first drafts from scraps—images, sounds—that have lodged in my mind and won't let go. Later, I look hard at what I've written in my notebook to see if a draft does all it can to explore (or exploit) what attracted my attention. As Mandelstam so brilliantly said, when a poem hangs around in your mind, you know it isn't finished (or words to that effect). For me, finding the right ending is often the reason a poem won't let go, although sometimes the middle needs more work so the true ending can emerge. Often a new idea for an unfinished poem will come when I'm *not*-thinking: walking, driving, washing dishes. At other times, looking harder at a draft, and listening to it, will reveal its heart. Occasionally, what a poem is really trying to say will appear only after I've thought it was finished.

For this anthology, I wanted first to look at a fairly recent poem in the light of one written almost thirty years earlier, both using the same central image—of horseback riding, which was a central feature of my childhood. The early poem, called "To My Mother," grew out of a conflicted relationship with my mother and was prompted by a photograph of my mother at twelve or thirteen holding her pony's halter and smiling at the camera. What struck me was how different she looked from the well-groomed, well-dressed matron I'd known all my life: her hair thick and wild, her patched coat too short for her dress, her riding boots scuffed, her grin one of absolute joy at being there, *in* her life, not answering to anyone. She, in fact, reminded me of myself in the present.

I remembered her stories of defying her strict grandmothers—in charge when her mother was sick or away—answering *I don't care* when they scolded. And I remembered my aunt, her older sister, saying once, "Your mother was a fearless rider," years away from the worrying mother I had always known. To explore the mysteries of change over time, I began by describing how she looked in the old photograph, making explicit the identification I saw, and imagining her joy in riding, the freedom she felt. My approach was direct—I was just beginning to write seriously, in my last semester at Goddard—and the poem's crucial question—"When did you start / to be afraid"—was naked, plainspoken.

The issue I wrestled with was how to end the poem with what Stanley Kunitz has called "a door and a window," wanting to find an image that would offer a depth of association that intellect and will couldn't provide. In imagining a turning point—how my mother might have felt when she lost her nerve for taking the highest fences—I express a self-revelatory empathy that I don't dwell on—"I think how doubt / like a falling leaf can flutter / at the corner of an eye"—but that leads (fairly organically, if pushed a bit, it must be said) to the image of a blurred scene becoming a wall. I was learning how to look, both at what inspired the poem and at the poem as it was lurching into light.

Twenty-five years later, prompted by my older granddaughter asking for "stories about when you were little," I began to deliberately explore childhood memories in poems, thinking of that younger self as a different person. What came first were horse (or pony) stories, one about why I stopped competitive riding that's almost a mirror of "To My Mother," but less direct, more compressed in syntax and sound, as well as more self-revealing. The act of writing, looking at the self as other, made possible more empathy than I could imagine in 1980.

CANTER

Lunge, torrent of muscle under me:
the horse lurched forward, I lurched
back, squinched, perched, precarious,
the saddle no help in the rush and bump
of this genteel gait short of a gallop
I must *master*, declared Mrs. Whit,
who believed her Christian Science—
that mind triumphs over matter—
insisting I have horsemanship
in my veins and must try every day
to ride as well as my mother.

No matter that my mother, her father,
older sister, younger brother all
meshed to their horses like Centaurs—
in the ring I was put in, bars

I had to clear, gripping harder
with shaking knees, exposed
to the sharp commands—*Head up,*
heels down—terror made me brave
enough to resist, no matter that if
I wouldn't be her pet project, her
miracle, I'd lose afternoons like that
last one in the barn, the sweet horse-
sweat smell as I curried damp fur,
the stall private and golden with dust,
the warm mare stalwart to lean against
as I watered and grained her, felt the graze
of horse lips, grace of a velvet nose.

More often than a change of vision over time, the delight or relief of insight
follows a nagging sense that a poem hasn't reached its potential or isn't alive to
begin with. I knew, even before my keen-eyed editor commented, "I think this
one could benefit from some condensing," that a poem originally called "Domain" plodded on the page. I was attached to the details, and at first thought
simple cuts would eliminate echoes of other poems in the manuscript.

DOMAIN [VERSION 1]

Her domain has emptied of all that was
here, all that was hers—the most ordinary
and the most intimate things:
the silver hairpin that matched her hair,
the cloth toy she'd fingered—*I'm sewing,*
but I don't know what for—unsure
if she was in this world, with its demands,
or the next: old woman or infant.

And emptied, the fortress from which
she faced the world shrinks:
only the curtains, stiff as sentries,
and the carpet she never replaced—
stained by the failing dog and then
by herself—left behind, a stage
where another life will play out now.

In the mirror now crated, carted
away, she worked to make her face
what it once was—fastening the wings
of her still thick hair with combs;
fastening gold at her throat, ears,
wrists—armor of the well-to-do.
She never, as they say, *let herself go,*
in all senses: good appearance
a mark of pride, or brave defiance
(though I didn't always see it
that way) of illness and age,
just as her mother wore pearls
with her nightgown when confined to bed.

The room as I turn to leave—empty
of the bed she lay on, the chest that held
the flimsy things she wore next her skin,
the chairs and chaise longue blooming
with chintz roses, the spindly desk
that for fifty years held the note: *I'M SORRY
I WAS BAD,* in my brother's crooked
block letters; the letter my father wrote
to his *Dearest,* telling her she'd done
a superb job with me; my effusions
from times away all boxed,
carted away—the room gives no sign
of the living and dying that went on here.

Towards the end, extreme-situation-only
petitioner, I prayed, *Don't let it get
worse,* and though it did, she escaped,
with our help, the worst,
stayed in this fortress, this domain,
until she slipped off her armor,
as it was being stripped from her,
and moved to another place.

After cutting many of the details that appear in other poems, I saw that the
syntax of stanza four was so overloaded by the set-off list that the subject had

to be repeated. The syntactic glitch showed that I'd tried to glide past the live wires in the poem: the written evidence in the desk. Also, I saw the exposure of my mother's final weaknesses as gratuitously graphic. The imagery of medieval defense, although psychologically accurate, seemed unsurprising and forced a predictable framework on the material. I scrapped the title for one perhaps too brutal, expressive of clearing the poem of its excess and obfuscation, although what happens after a death is hardly gentle. I chose the phrases that pleased me most in the earlier version and, in focusing on my father's letter, realized that the mystery of its having been hand delivered to its addressee was illuminated by something my mother had said after my father's death and that I had used in an earlier poem: "He never liked to talk about feelings."

CLEARING THE ROOM

Her bedroom has emptied of all that was
here, all that was hers—the most ordinary
and the most intimate things: the bed she lay
and died in; the chest that held the flimsy silks
she wore next her skin; the curtains and chairs
upholstered in roses; the spindly desk
that held its secrets fifty years—
the folded note *I'M SORRY I WAS BAD*
in my brother's crooked crayoned caps,
(Was he five? Six? what had he done?);
my letters of delight at being on my own, away;
and one from my father when I was eighteen,
not stamped or mailed, clearly delivered
by hand—by a man, as she said,
who *didn't like to talk*
about feelings, and wrote:
Dearest,

You've done a superb job with Joan—
I who didn't understand she was
working, didn't know how hard.

Elizabeth Arnold

Rhyme and Quantity in Free Verse

I have to confess, when writing a poem I don't know what I'm doing as I'm doing it, but something in me knows, and I think this something is the something in me that knows about music.

A central component of music in poems is rhyme, which along with the closely related quantity tends to be ignored in discussions of free verse.

Rhyme in my poems does not occur at regular intervals. The rhyme sounds do not always come at the ends of lines. Full rhyme is pretty rare, yet when it is not full it can be close to assonance and therefore pretty loud.

Other kinds of repeated or near-repeated sounds happen more frequently, something I think of as rhyme in the largest sense. This kind of rhyme produces a weave or web, the fabric of the poem, physically speaking. It affects the sense in subtle but very important ways.

For example, a string of words can begin with a single vowel sound or related vowel sounds, creating a sense of vulnerability, as if the words have taken their clothes off. The effect of this kind of rhyme is more intense when the words are monosyllabic, which can lead to a useful counterpoint between short and long words, usually Germanic versus Latinate words, calling attention to how some syllables take longer to pronounce than others, which is duration or quantity. To my ear, quantity is determined mostly by what the consonants of a word or syllable are doing, but sometimes vowels can affect it.

I'll talk a little about how all of this links up with the sense in some of my poems.

HEART VALVE

They told me there'd be pain

so when I felt it,
sitting at my beat-up farm desk

that looks out glass doors

onto the browning garden—plain sparrows
bathing in the cube-shaped fountain

so violently they drain it,

the white-throats with their
wobbly two-note song

on the long way south still,

and our dogs
out like lights and almost

falling off their chairs

freed of the real-time for awhile
as time began for me

to swell, slow down, carry me out

of all this almost
to a where

about as strong a lure as love.

A prominent feature of this poem is its use of extended syntax. In fact, the poem appears to be a single sentence but never completes itself, which enacts the resistance to ending (in this case dying) that the poem is about.

But rhyme is also very alive in the poem and for the same reason. There is some full rhyme early on: *pain, plain, drain.* The word *drain* might be the most important word in the poem, and the rhyme calls attention to it. Brutal almost, relentless, *drain* echoes the "beat-up farm desk," which is an early stand-in for the speaker's body. This tough feeling persists to the end of the poem, where the near-alliteration of vowels in "out // of all this almost" creates its own brand of physicality with the emphasis syllable to syllable, while at the same time conveying a sense of vulnerability just at the moment the poem makes its final push beyond a bodily this-world perspective, the "this almost."

Another crucial sound contained in those first full rhyme words and elsewhere in the poem is the *n* sound (*pain, plain, drain* and *when, sitting, onto, browning, garden, bathing, violently*). The *n* sound is important here because it lengthens the time it takes to pronounce a syllable, increasing its quantity. In the context of this poem, such lengthening amplifies the avoidance of ending that's set up by the syntax.

As does the *l* sound, and it's everywhere: *told, felt, looks, glass, plain,* violently coming before *drain,* and after that also: *wobbly, long, still,* [*like, lights*], *almost, falling, real, awhile,* [*swell, slow*], [*all, almost*], [*lure, love*]. I've bracketed those words with *l* sounds that are close together or even adjacent, which happens more often as the poem progresses. And I could have done the same with words containing an *n* sound and words that have both one or more *l* sounds *and n* sounds: *plain, violently, long, falling.* Double-whammy words quantity-wise.

Vowels can have this lengthening effect also, as in the case of diphthongs or near-diphthongs in words like *real* and *lure* and *valve* where one-syllable words sound like they have two syllables. I wonder how much the *l* sound is adding to this effect. Still, the lengthening seems to be happening within the vowel, not the consonants, as versus a word like *plain.*

I thought I'd look next at a fragment—rock in the stream of the ever-moving language, just as staccato words like *beat-up* and *white-throats* almost halt the legato flow of a one-sentence poem, emphasizing movement by contrast.

DADDY

> . . . never seeming closer than when wordless,
> heavy shape of meaning, prehistoric.

When he dived, he didn't hold his hands in front
so that the head hit first, blunt.
His whole being like that.

Just as "Heart Valve" seems to be desperate to keep moving, darting toward
and away from its subject, the movement of the language itself enacting the poem's subject, "Daddy" must stop, like a fist hitting a concrete wall. And again, as
in "Heart Valve," the most prominent rhyme of the poem, the full rhyme of *blunt*
with *front*, emphasizes this idea—by way of the repetition of course but also by
way of the nature of the rhyme sound itself. There are the elongating *n* sounds,
yes, but the *t* sound hampers fluidity, calling a halt to it. The *that* of the last line
settles any doubt on this score, as do, to my ear anyway, the four heavily stressed
monosyllabic words that end the penultimate line, three of which end with *t*, the
fourth with another concussive sound, *d*. That these words are adjacent to each
other is important and that the line is solidly end-stopped: "head hit first, blunt."

Another short poem enacts its content by way of the texture of the language.
Although rhyme calls attention to itself early, the poem does not crescendo
rhyme-wise until the third couplet.

LOOKING AT MAPS

If they'd had writing in time, Cuba could have been Crete,
watery source of the Minoans and thus the Greeks.

What's lost? A possible us
growing like new foliage out of stony ground, emerging?

Last voice, first, a whole world calling—
awful, inaudible—into the unstoppable loud (roaring!)

hurricane-force sea wind.

There's a lot happening musically in line two. The almost full end-rhyme
comes close to eclipsing a blurring effect of the first half that echoes the movement of water itself—I think quantity is at the bottom of this, with *watery* and
Minoans longer than the cut-off *Greeks* that rhymes with *Crete*.

But more important is the climax of panic, even horror, that dominates the third couplet and how the sound of the language amps this idea. The broad *a* sound in *call-*, *aw-*, and *-au-* is at the heart of this. And that *-ful* and *-ble* in those last two words make a full rhyme underscoring the idea that something inaudible can be awful—not just unpleasant, but carrying a biblical enormity. All of this happens at a very high speed, increasing its force. I hear a little bit of the *aw* sound in the second syllable of *unstoppable*, which ends with another rhyme sound woven through this passage, *-ble*. So *calling, awful, inaudible,* and *unstoppable* produce a crescendo of association by way of an increasing density of rhyme.

I think the *au* sound takes longer to say, reminding me of a voice actually calling—across centuries in this case.

Bringing me back to this whole business of the lengthened syllable and to my last poem, which begins by describing the sound of a person's voice coming over the radio. The length of time it took for the person to say a one-syllable word spawns a meditation on the fragility of civilization.

CIVILIZATION

The British journalist's voice was spent as she said
(unenthusiastically,

the interview now over), "Thanks," with the eager
young insatiable American official

turning, then, to other matters. But the voice,
a European's—flat, well schooled

in the world's hope-pulverizing particle storm's
gifts of disappointment—stayed,

the syllable's slight elongation
something on the order of

the querulous sendings of frail human wonderings out
into the void, as if the waning

of her voice spoke all of history's ups and downs,
a honey-comb's packed maze of cells

whose lights shine through their little paper membranes
too thin not to be available

to being torn, light leaking from a world cracked open,
sky seen through the pavement I walk down.

The funny thing is, the word *thanks* doesn't normally take very long to say, in spite of that *n*, so the poem has to go to great lengths to describe what is making this pretty quick word last in the mind of the speaker, creating an opportunity for the poet. That the word is spoken in a "querulous" manner partly explains why the journalist would hold onto the word a little longer. The line that conveys this idea best performs what it's describing, carrying us slowly across the page: "the querulous sendings of frail human wonderings out." The *n* sounds mostly but also the *l* sounds contribute to the line's increased quantity. And then this fragile thinking, this wondering that seems to be floating its long way across, slams into "the void"—a hard sound, a hard fact.

That collision—which the sounds of the words make physical—amplifies the tone of resignation, setting off a consideration of history. The syntactic convolutions of the description of paper membranes as "too thin not to be available / to being torn" continues the development of a feeling of fear that drives the poem (and includes its share of *n* and *l* sounds). That anything would make itself available to being destroyed—as if willingly—this is disturbing, and that we are forever hurting each other and ourselves, and how this extends to that of nations and whole civilizations over millennia. The time it takes to pronounce the syllables is annealed to what it is to be a mind in the process of thinking these things.

As a writer of poems, I think of a word often because it rhymes with something that's come before. I think of one way of saying something—one of many—because this one way of saying something uses sounds already present in the ear. The poem catches hold of its subject, snagging the reader (and the writing writer) by involving itself in the sounds of words in interaction with their meanings. One thing is emphasized over another. It all happens by intuition but at the same time it happens with a purpose, a certain kind of focus.

Martha Rhodes

Unplanned Sequences

THE SMALL CANAL BETWEEN THEM

Into the small canal is Nothing

ever tossed? This is a dare-not-
venture-into place
and so persists, tannic and idle

for the rest of their lives.

IT FELL ON ME

It fell on me to write his stone,
purchased before I was born,
along with my mother's.
Easy to write hers. *Loving Mother of Me.*
But for him—what? beyond his name
and dates—four years since
the marble company asked me
for the words I wished inscribed.
It was never my ambition
to be the good daughter.
Was, though, to be

my husband's good wife.
And now, he's silent too—

and the western reaches of the bed,
his side, stay light, and a fault line
divides our small plot. What
to chisel into our marriage stone?
That he just regarded me as that
which he wished lived elsewhere?

Erasure. Dunes rising, and even
shorter days in the east.

COME TO ME, HIS BLOOD

Come to me, his blood,
so I may cup you,
be reservoir and ladle, both—
clean, store, and stir.
Then serve you back to him.

Come to me, his blood, ill,
so I may warm, sieve, and funnel
you back to him; his cheeks ruddy
again, his head in my lap.
The wind is up! and sails our boat

across Farm Pond, our friends
on shore waving us to picnic time—
a hammock-nap, a swim—
all four of us, all well.
Not dozens of summers ago,

but now, this final Sunday in July,
come to me, his blood. Don't rush
onto a lawn or street, don't seep—
but if you do leave him, if spilt,
you who cannot slow or thicken

redirect yourself—you must—come to me
and I will bring you back to him.

THROMBOSIS

A rat carried this week to us between its teeth and dropped
it at our feet and not even our youngest cat sniffed at it,
though the rat surely left his scent on each day, morning
through night. And the rat will find its way to us here, too,
where at the hospital I hold onto your foot lest you
be rolled away without me. We fear the rat will bring more
Weeks of Inability, both of us unable—though today I am
able to eat every doughnut New York City offers.
My grandfather was a baker from Vienna.
Perhaps he'd say to me today, *Doughnuts are in your blood.*
And what should I say about your blood, dear, not knowing
yet what's in your blood that brings us here this week.

THE CONCUSSION

Let me remind you that the bile
his injury riled up arrived
on your pillow as you slept.

He would have forgotten
the shower's purpose
were you not there,
soaping him front and back,
your hair not clean yet, braided
and complicated to unbraid
when wet and foul;
the bed hastily stripped
then re-made by you
while he, propped in a chair
and snug in your robe,
stared at—
what—

For all of this, he still
may not be kind to you again—
concussions known to turn some rabid.

Your floppy retriever. Now he's weaving
toward coffee in the galley kitchen.
Retract your hand.

While I have never set out to write a poetic sequence, it has turned out, thus
far, that I have ended up writing book-length sequences. I don't necessarily an-
nounce my books as such, but I hope, of course, that readers will read them—as
they should any collection, sequence or not—from first to last page so that the
effort that I've put into organizing the work will pay off for the reader. In other
words, the poem on page 10, say, is informed by pages 1–9, and these poems
prepare readers for what is to come.

I am very earnest when I say that I don't set out to write linked poems. The
poems come, one by one, over the course of several years, and as I write them,
and as they accumulate, I begin to recognize that they are working with and off
of each other. The individual poem usually arrives first through music, through
one word attaching to another, then another. Story and emotional narratives
reveal themselves to me over time.

For this anthology, I have selected poems that are situated at the beginning of
my fourth collection, *The Beds*. They set the stage for a book that comes out of
domestic upheaval, illness, and dis-ease with partner, self, other(s), and place.
"Come to Me, His Blood" surprised me for its "stiffness" of telling, its rather
arch tone. It surprised me but felt quite right for a frenzy that revolves around a
blood disorder, where fluidity is very much at issue. It resonates with the book's
first poem, "The Small Canal Between Them"—is not a canal an artery?— and
with the blood clot that threatens in "Thrombosis" and, a few pages past, with
the galley kitchen (another artery) of "The Concussion" where the speaker's
beloved turns, temperamentally, rabid dog and weaves toward coffee—and the
speaker. And of course, the narrowness, or compression, or pressure of the canal, and of the arteries that hold the blood that threatens to spill, and of the
thrombosis that threatens to burst, and of the narrow kitchen through which
the rabid blood of the beloved courses, resonates with the fault line, the ultimate
pressure point, that splits the two sides of the marital bed in "It Fell on Me."

Revelation and insight come to us as we progress from title, to first word of
first line of poem, to the last word of the last poem of a collection. As I become
more familiar with my work over time, as I live deeply in it, I start to see how
the poems cooperate with each other, or rub against each other, through image,
narrative, tone, and temperature.

Jennifer Grotz

The Expressive Use of Landscape

"Feelings, oh I have those," goes a poem I love, "They govern me." The poem, however, is spoken by a field of poppies, and it comes from Louise Glück's *The Wild Iris*, a foundational book for me exactly for its use of landscape and speaker to think about subjectivity, the human's position in the world, the role of art, and the will of God. It's a poem that must surely point to the "little hell flames" of Sylvia Plath's "Poppies in July," the poppies Plath describes as "little bloody skirts" or like mouths:

> And it exhausts me to watch you
> Flickering like that, wrinkly and clear red, like the skin of a mouth.
> . . .
> If I could bleed, or sleep!——
> If my mouth could marry a hurt like that!

As a very young poet, I admonished myself for writing like Plath and strove not to sound like her. As much as I loved the hot-bloodedness of her poems, at times I felt they were dangerously narcissistic. And then there was the gender question, by which I mean my own nervous ambivalence over how I had encountered other people read Plath's work so closely in terms of the feminine and as a sort of counterpart to an otherwise masculine poetry. "Every woman poet must go through Plath," my first poetry teacher told me. (Male poets were allowed other prepositions—to go around, over, before, etc. . . .) In any case, as a young poet, I imposed my own private interdiction against her influence, and I took as a model instead the decided cold-bloodedness of Wallace Stevens's figure of the snowman. How I loved the assertion that by paying careful attention, by allowing oneself to be "cold for a long time," one could hear the sad howl of the wind as something else entirely! Imagistically speaking, Stevens's snowman, blended perfectly into the landscape surrounding him, achieved something I infinitely wished: to be objective.

Then again, to be objective is not truly to be a human at all, Stevens's poem equally suggests. And yet, a veering toward that coolness seems worthwhile at the very least as a method to view the world accurately, on its own terms. And so like a painter, over and over in poems I have started with the intention— instead of expressing my inchoate interior, an impulse I find impossible fully to achieve or to extinguish—that I would describe and render the exterior world. And what the poems seem often to focus upon is neither the "objective" nor the "subjective" reality of what's being described but some consciousness about where and how those two realms—the human and the natural—overlap. When I describe the landscape, what am I describing? the poems seem to query. And what is there waiting to be seen?

I suppose, like most things in poems, what I've discovered developing is a sort of eros: that way a poem captures a temporary and intensified expression of the *relation* between human and nature, not a choosing between the two. And over time, I have felt something like a lover's affection and gratitude to the world itself, phenomenally expressive and just as worthwhile and certainly as plea- surable to perceive as the feelings that govern my human realm. Finally, though I think I will never stop trying to see and describe the world more adequately, more accurately—so many poppies quivering in the wind, so many different- sized moths at the lamp!—I now understand that regardless, humans still need the world to help describe and therefore to see and to understand ourselves.

LANDSCAPE WITH OSPREY AND SALMON

Rain ticks upon the ferns, over which
if you listen carefully, the osprey's cries
alert the others that it's found the salmon,
now colored ash with rot and dragged to rocks

where the bird pulls at the elastic flesh.
Another salmon skeleton draped upon a log
hangs like a feather boa left out in the rain
and the skin that once contained it has slid off

like something silk. Rapture joins the world
and irony divides, and unaware of either
the osprey desperately undresses every bone
and then unbuttons both the eyes.

THE FIELD

There was a dirt field I'd walk to as a girl,
past the convenience store and the train tracks
where the day laborers congregated with six-packs,
where the two-lane road turned to one lane with yellow stripes
and the vacant field loomed like a desiccated fallen sky.

That's where I'd go to sit on an oblong rock
until prairie dogs sprouted from tunnels underground
and the ground became a fabric
stitched by fluid lines of ants.
And though barely perceptible,

if I waited long enough,
the world would begin its shallow breathing,
the soundless wind's only duty in that field
to rearrange a few grains of sand
while the smell of hot dust grew sharp in the nose.

I waited. I don't know for what.
Sometimes I'd sit so long the sun would sink,
a fiery stare blinking shut beneath the horizon,
and the drooping electric wires would borrow the dark
until the dark seeped back into the sky. And when stars

surfaced like needles piercing through velvet,
I'd hold myself back just a moment more.
What made me feel watched in the naked field?
I was paying close attention and could discern only
a begging to be cloaked and a begging to be released.

THE JETTY

It is incorrect to say, "The dark clouds above
bloom full-blown roses." Unless
superbly engorged roses are terrifying to you,
and fascinating, but also ordinary,

in fact, hardly seen. And here, on this jetty
that points toward the blue abyss
where freight ships disappear,

it is imprecise to say the gulf water sings,
that it is a very old song
roughly sung this rainy afternoon. Because here
there is no music, just a soft monotonous roar
the waves spill across the rocks, a liquefaction of lace,
I think, though I know the water's cold and mindless,
that the waves touch blindly, that they continue
like desire, forcing forward until spent.

But if you follow the stray cat
that picks his way upon the rocks
to the beach where the sandpipers run forward to the edge of wet
left when the waves withdraw
                                    then hop backward
when the waves rush in, it will be precise to say
that an afternoon is when what it was you had wanted turns
unfamiliar. And when the rain
percusses across the jetty, mixing with the waves
until it seems to be falling upward,
it will be correct to state
that the tall beach grasses lean down
because all day the wind subdues them.

POPPIES

There is a sadness everywhere present
but impossible to point to, a sadness that hides in the world
and lingers. You look for it because it is everywhere.
When you give up, it haunts your dreams
with black pepper and blood and when you wake
you don't know where you are.

But then you see the poppies, a disheveled stand of them.
And the sun shining down like God, loving all of us equally,

mountain and valley, plant, animal, human, and therefore
shouldn't we love all things equally back?
And then you see the clouds.

The poppies are wild, they are only beautiful and tall
so long as you do not cut them,
they are like the feral cat who purrs and rubs against your leg
but will scratch you if you touch back.
Love is letting the world be half-tamed.
That's how the rain comes, softly and attentively, then

with unstoppable force. If you
stare upwards as it falls, you will see
they are falling sparks that light nothing only because
the ground interrupts them. You can hear the way they'd burn,
the smoldering sound they make falling into the grass.

That is a sound for the sadness everywhere present.
The closest you have come to seeing it
is at night, with the window open and the lamp on,
when the moths perch on the white walls,
tiny as a fingernail to large as a Gerber daisy,
and take turns agitating around the light.

If you grasp one by the wing,
its pill-sized body will convulse
in your closed palm and you can feel the wing beats
like an eyelid's obsessive blinking open to see.
But now it is still light and the blackbirds are singing
like their voices are the only scissors left in this world.

Maurice Manning

Honky Tankas

THE BACK WOODS RUCKUS

Today I woke the crows;
how they squalled at me.
How I called back, You,
Peckerwoods!—You, Yahoo! they followed.
I'm welling up remembering: trees
hooded, suddenly bald, sad toodle-oo.

THE PERSIMMON TREE

I shook the tree alright,
troubling it for two persimmons.

Were they symbolic hanging there,
reddish flecks ticking the sky?

And wasn't the man, shinnied
half way up, another symbol?

THE TIN ROOF THE BIRDSONG AND THE RAIN

When that washboard clacks; when
someone whistles with it, washing
the sky; when a worksong

wakes me up, Damn you,
I think. You shoulda oughta.
What, marry a long woman?

THE LAST PONE GONE, A SWALLER IN THE KETTLE

Well, I was sitting there
drinking pot likker left from
a mess of beans. Something

come over me. Sakes no!
not hardly his presence, but
God Almighty, he was close.

THE WORD FOLLER AND OTHERS LIKE IT

O, come along behind, heel
up close, hear? Let's foller

the holler's moon glint stream,
rushy as a woman's hair

set how? Aloose!—God's dream
goes thisaway, hindways his finger.

A couple of years ago in correspondence with a student, I found myself rambling on and on about lyricism. I was drawing attention to the suddenness and
the sudden coherence of lyric expression; I mentioned something about the
way a lyric poem tracks the Self in process, in process of seeking, discovering,
completing: a Self that has been prompted—implicitly—and is on its way. I
even ventured to consider that there may be degrees of lyricism within the same
poem, one mode that feels descriptive and one that feels interpretive, emphasizing that both modes are inherently emotive and occasionally cross paths with
each other, thus making a kind of triangulation in the poem between description, interpretation, and the fusion of the two. But what did I know! Soon after
initiating this conversation about lyricism, I realized I had climbed considerably
out on a limb, because I typically write narrative poems. Yes, even narrative po-

ems contain lyric moments, probably of necessity, but I knew I hadn't given sufficient thought to lyricism and wanted—as a kind of admonishment—to back myself into a corner from which I had to confront that brightly burning creature with yellow eyes and let it sing.

And so the corner I made for myself became a stanza consisting of thirty words—six lines, five words per line. I decided I'd allow the odd-numbered lines to begin with a basically iambic rise and let the even-numbered lines stumble along on rough-hewn trochaic footing. I even allowed room for some off-beat rhyme. Somewhere in the process of developing this little stanza I decided I wanted to use three rhetorical brush strokes—three seemed a simple number, and it's also an odd number, which clashes with the even numbers in the stanza, the six lines and the thirty words; the prospect of jamming together odd and even numbers had great appeal. This business with the word count, the six lines, the metrical step and lurch, the clumsy rhyming, and the rhetorical parrying has a very basic purpose—it gives the stanza a firm structure. It's also probably cheating, in the sense that I've dropped the dependable structural features of narrative that for me have always been scenic and dramatic and internal to the mode and replaced them with a system of structure that feels more external. It's notable, too, that these little poems still retain plenty of narrative stuff, and over the course of a manuscript they have a cumulative effect, and so I wonder if I've yet written a purely lyrical poem. But that has become less and less my concern. I've become content to write as openly as possible within the confines of a tight form—and the push of that impulse toward openness against rigid form seems to be a quality of lyricism.

Finally, these thirty-word poems tend to "begin" with a consideration of a naturally expressive word or phrase, particularly words associated with a rural vernacular. I've always liked the phrase "pot likker," and I've always admired anyone who says "foller" instead of "follow." Vernacular strikes me as inherently lyrical not simply because it refuses to be proper but also because it evokes its own world, and that separate world occurring beyond the page seems always to lie in the path of lyricism. After hearing a few of these little numbers Brooks Haxton declared they were *honky tankas*, not proper tankas, of course, but nevertheless a description I have found to be instructive as I continue with them. I'm grateful to Brooks for this description and for much more.

Mark Jarman

Sonnets, Holy and Unholy

SOFTEN THE BLOW, IMAGINED GOD, AND GIVE

Soften the blow, imagined God, and give
Me one good reason for this punishment.
Where does the pressure come from? Is it meant
To kill me in the end or help me live?
My thoughts about you are derivative.
Still, I believe a part of me is bent
To make your grace look like an accident
And keep my soul from being operative.
But if I'm to be bent back like the pole
A horseshoe clangs against and gives a kink to,
Then take me like the grinning iron monger
I saw once twist a bar that made him sink to
His knees. His tongue was like a hot pink coal
As he laughed and said he thought that he was stronger.

Mark Jarman, *Unholy Sonnets*
("Batter My Heart, Three-Person'd God"
John Donne, *Holy Sonnets*)

I CAN'T DO MORE THAN THIS. I CAN'T DO LESS—

I can't do more than this. I can't do less—
To choose a target adamant as death
And try to find a way to make it bend.
Try faith and insult. Even try to bless

Annihilation for its selflessness.
Try cool indifference. Try a lust for life.
Blue smoke by day and mirror-fire by night.
Try forcing imagination to confess,
In the strict silence of the infinite spaces,
That it was made for filling in the blanks,
For drawing features on the empty faces,
Including death's, and reading them like books.
Try reading, then, the writing on the face
That blunts immortal and industrial diamonds.

pers017catich

Mark Jarman, *Unholy Sonnets*
("Death, Be Not Proud"
John Donne, *Holy Sonnets*)

WHAT WILL WE GIVE UP IN THE AFTER LIFE

What will we give up in the after life,
When we have been enhanced to a higher power
And all the goodness of the body made so pure
Its quantum leap will have to feel like loss?
In our spirit flesh, *pneumatikon*
(Though the Greek sounds like a mattress); to see
Will be to take; to wish for, have; to sigh
Will be the sign of utter satisfaction.
But what about that instant of desire
Before we're gratified, the rapturous waiting
On this side of epiphany and climax?
Without the lapse of time, we'll lose that pleasure,
The unique arousal of previsioning,
The thrill in scenting that first cup of coffee.

what incuse

Mark Jarman, *Unholy Sonnets*
("I Am a Little World Made Cunningly"
John Donne, *Holy Sonnets*)

IN VIA EST CISTERNA

All she remembers from her Latin class
Is a phrase she echoes for her granddaughter.
Lately I hear in everything she says
A depth that she covers up with laughter.
In the road is a well. But in her mind
It fills with blanks, like a shaft of sand and pebbles.   pocket
A well is in the road. It is profound,   with
I'm sure, it is a phrase with many levels.   holes"
And then, I see one: the woman with five husbands
Met Jesus there. But my mother had only one—
Unless now having lost him she understands
That he was never who she thought, but someone
Who was different men with different women through the years.
In the road is a well. It fills with tears.

Mark Jarman, *Unholy Sonnets*
("Since She Whom I Lov'd Hath Paid her Last Debt"
John Donne, *Holy Sonnets*)

John Donne (1572–1631), born Roman Catholic in a dangerous time and place
to be one, in late Elizabethan England, and relatively well off, traveled the world
as a soldier, was known as a bit of a lad, a dandy and a ladies' man, and a poet of
wit and sensuality and erotic pleasure. In 1600 he was poised for a diplomatic
career, as secretary to Sir Thomas Egerton, Lord Keeper of the Great Seal, and
made the mistake of falling in love with his boss's niece Anne More, married
her in secret against her uncle's and father's wishes, and ruined his career. Even
ended up in prison for a spell. He lived in a kind of internal exile in the country-
side with his wife and family for a dozen years, working as a lawyer, and finally
gaining favor with King James, who would reinstate him at court, but only if he
took holy orders. That meant totally repudiating his original faith. He did so in
1615 and was ordained into the Church of England. The last sixteen years of his
life he was very prominent in the church and held the post of dean or rector of
St. Paul's Cathedral from 1620 until his death.

During the period of being out of favor and a little beyond, between 1609
and 1617, he wrote what we call the Holy Sonnets. As religious meditations,
they are anything but consoling or complacent. They reflect the turmoil of the

changes in his life, living in poverty, trying to support a growing family, watching children die and ultimately his wife die of childbirth, and all the while the poems offer us a highly intelligent poet of metaphorical inventiveness and subtlety arguing with God, acting as if God could be reasoned with, and finding his way into the orthodoxy of a new belief that saw itself as existing between the divine hierarchy of the Roman church and the individual emphasis of Calvinist Protestantism. The poems are blazing monuments of intellectual fire written during an ongoing crisis of faith.

When Donne began writing his sonnets, the sonnet form, an Italian import, had been popular among English poets for about one hundred years. It arrived at the court of Henry VIII and caught on quickly among the court poets and wits. For one hundred years its subject was secular or courtly love, with some diversions into other pursuits, like the desire for fame, but always earthly. Donne changed that. But he preserved the form's dialectical structure, in which an idea or condition is proposed in the first eight lines or octave, and then a counterargument is made in the final six lines. Though he observed the Italian rhyme scheme of the octave (a b b a a b b a), he frequently combined it with the rhyme scheme of the last six lines of an English sonnet (c d c d e e).

Donne published none of his poems during his lifetime (though he did publish sermons and various tracts). Still they were widely known, because the means of publication among his circle was to pass manuscripts around or to copy new poems out by hand and distribute them. Though Donne's sonnets do recount a crisis of faith, they are orthodox in their resolutions. To be otherwise was not a good idea. Those who read Donne's sonnets, though they might have been shocked by some of their matter, would have grasped their spirit and approved. That is, Donne could be sure that his readers believed as he did.

I had reached a critical point in my religious belief. It was nowhere near as momentous as John Donne's, though I believe anyone's crisis of faith is dramatic to that person. I wanted to learn what I might really believe, and I wanted to do this by writing poetry, particularly a very formal and traditional kind of verse that would be intellectually demanding and would challenge me. I thought I would simply write responses to each of John Donne's nineteen Holy Sonnets. This project didn't last long. He was a Jacobean genius. I was only a contemporary American poet who had become estranged over the years from my Christianity. What I learned, however, as I wrote—and I wrote well over one hundred sonnets, preserving about half of them for two different books (*Questions for Ecclesiastes* and *Unholy Sonnets*)—was that the sonnet could be an effective devotional form. Every day for several years I sat down to work on a sonnet, sometimes in response to a Donne sonnet, as with the first two presented here, which are direct responses to two of his most famous Holy Sonnets ("Batter My Heart, Three-Person'd God" and "Death, Be Not Proud"). And though the subsequent two I've included do have original models in Donne's Holy Sonnets, more often I was simply responding to an aspect of belief that had arisen in my life or an event that caused me to question belief in some fundamental way. The fourth of the poems I've included, "*In via est cisterna*," has to do with my mother's sorrow over her divorce, and seeing that Donne had written one of his Holy Sonnets on the occasion of his wife's death ("Since She Whom I Lov'd Hath Paid her Last Debt") gave me permission to write in a similarly elegiac way.

Every day when I stopped working on one of these sonnets, I realized I had understood a little more about faith. I called my poems Unholy Sonnets as a way of warding off piety and orthodoxy, even as a way of suggesting a tendency to be unorthodox if not exactly sacrilegious or blasphemous. Thus while some are strictly Italian or English in form, others depart in rhyme scheme or meter or both from these traditional models. I wanted to invite readers who might not be believers into a poem that would surprise them with its serious religious concerns. The irony would be that irony itself would be peeled away like a mask. The poems would reveal themselves as fundamentally sincere.

Alan Williamson

Two Public Poems

The idea of a capacious public poetry that would not be mere editorializing, propaganda, or preaching to the choir has fascinated me since the 1960s, and I've discussed it a great deal in my critical writing. But my own more ambitious public poems have not been acts of will. They have come on me out of the blue and always with a panicky feeling, "Could anyone carry this off?" None more so, of course, than the idea of what amounted to a public ceremony, or liturgy, for nuclear disarmament.

"Recitation for the Dismantling of a Hydrogen Bomb" was written at the time of the Reagan-era arms race, the time of Jonathan Schell's *The Fate of the Earth*. Fear of nuclear war had perhaps never been more widespread since the Cuban Missile Crisis. (To be fair, we did not then know of Reagan's absolute determination not to wage a nuclear war or of his long-term plans, judicious or not, for coercing the Soviet Union into making peace.) Half of America watched the ABC-TV movie about the aftermath of a nuclear war, *The Day After*. Later a friend, who considered the movie "trashy," expressed the wish that I wouldn't give it so much credit for the genesis of my poem. But some of its images—the wristwatch on the bedside table that rattles when the missiles take off, then goes on ticking—had seared themselves indelibly into my imagination. Finally, it seemed to me appropriate that a poem intended as a collective act should draw on popular as well as high culture.

The poem was not concerned with blaming anyone or anything, beyond "our tireless fear of each other," for the nuclear predicament. But it did want to acknowledge two disturbing truths: that we could never undo the *knowledge* of how to make nuclear weapons, whatever we did with the bombs themselves; and that it to some degree goes against human nature to have a power and not to use it. Two contexts, both far from the political, helped me to approach these questions with some margin of hope.

My old friend Jon Kabat-Zinn had just started the Stress Reduction Clinic at the University of Massachusetts Medical Center, using meditation and yoga to help people live with chronic pain conditions conventional medicine had given up on. My wife, who had suffered for years from back and knee problems, was in a parallel program run by Dr. Herbert Benson at Beth Israel Hospital in Boston. Though I wasn't a meditator yet myself, her accounts of the day-long retreats, and their evident effect on her state of mind, sank into me deeply. This entered into the poem, not only as an intuitive image of hope but as a metaphor: could our capacity for collective self-destruction be a kind of chronic pain, which we could learn to live with if only we ceased futilely to wish it out of existence?

The other context was the end of Bach's St. Matthew Passion, where the chorus sings "Good night" to the dead Jesus in the tomb, after the soloist has vowed to bury Him within his own heart. That this Christian masterwork ended not with the Resurrection but with the sealing of the stone of the tomb had always moved me profoundly. It even resonated distantly with the Death-of-God theologians' paradoxical argument that only in entertaining the possibility of God's nonexistence could we participate fully in the loneliness, the absolute self-sacrifice, of Christ on the cross. All this spoke to my sense of the terrible uniqueness of our collective existential position; and I hoped it was not blasphemous to give it the further torque—audible only in one or two verbal echoes—of applying it to the feelings we might have on taking back the godlike power we had presumed to into the depths of our own minds:

> not only that nothing
> any longer overarched us, but that we
> must contain what had.

Rilke says someplace that the circumstances of an entire lifetime may exist "for the sake of a single poem." And I'm not unaware that public poems are often most successful when they turn to imagery outside the expected realm: Lowell's aquarium and underground parking garage in "For the Union Dead," C. K. Williams's roofers in "Tar." For myself, I can only say that without these two circumstances my poem would never have found its way to a resolution.

I will admit to fudging one thing. My research skills are not the best, and I couldn't find any unclassified account of how one would actually go about dismantling a hydrogen bomb. I learned what I could about the bomb's inner structure and took it apart, one layer at a time.

I did continue, throughout, to think of the poem as a "recitation," as something that not everyone, perhaps, but a large number of people could say communally. I'm not the kind of poet who normally thinks very much about "audience," except in terms of rudimentary clarity—assuming that what rings true to me will ring true to at least some other people. But in this case I was careful about what was eccentric, what could be generally agreed to. A couple of grim lines about overpopulation were cut because one friend felt he couldn't imagine himself saying them, though others had liked them. I didn't actually think the poem would be recited ceremonially; but my rule was to write it as if it *could.*

In some ways, writing public poems gets more difficult as one gets older. One wonders whether the degree of alienation one feels from the ways the world has changed is worth setting down on paper or is simply the crotchetiness of every old man in every age. The suspicion, for instance, that the saturating presence of the media, poststructuralist thought, the "posthuman," might be eroding our sense of our own reality, in the body and the moment, in an unprecedented way. . . . While I was thinking these thoughts I was reading a good deal of Louis-Ferdinand Celine, a writer in bad odor up to his death for some anti-Semitic pamphlets he wrote just before World War II (though he never, as far as I could find out, actually collaborated with the Germans). What interested me about Celine was not his past but the almost hysterical voice with which he chronicled his wanderings with his wife and cat across Europe during and just after the end of the war. Only that voice seemed adequate to the enormity of what he had seen. What, I wondered, would his black humor have made of our world? Might he, for instance, have found the case of two teenagers in Tacoma, hit from behind by a train because they couldn't hear anything above the sound of their Walkmans, grimly emblematic? One day, waking up from a nap, I half-heard his voice handing on to me an insult directed at him in prison; and the poem was off and running.

I suppose part of it was the freedom not to try to seem likeable, as Celine was hardly a likeable man, though often, in his private life, a generous and compassionate one. Passages I had written and found stiff and self-righteous in my own voice came to life, peppered with his characteristic exclamation points, intercut with direct quotes from some of his lesser-known works. Many unexpected things sprang out—even a bawdy multilingual pun on Vergil's Latin!

Celine's voice allowed me a wider range of opinions than one might express in normal conversation. One might, for instance, in the aftermath of 9/11, hate *both* radical Islam and capitalist globalization. One might both believe and disbelieve a friend's conspiracy theory, figuring that, in the whirlwind of information and disinformation, it was impossible to know anyway and that the world was equally terrible in either case. And, of course, he had to attack *me*, as part of the world he held in contempt.

Celine's voice allowed me to put forth a dark imaginative truth about our current world (it's also a poem about ecology), without asking the reader either to take it literally or to get it entangled with his/her opinion of me, if s/he has one. I codedicated the poem to Robert Pinsky, because the jagged collages of his *Gulf Music* joined with Celine in giving me the idea.

Two poems, from relatively early and late in my career. I don't know what moral to draw in conclusion. Except, perhaps, that both were intended, beyond the realm of opinions, to do what poetry is uniquely suited to do: to plant in the reader's mind an emotional possibility, in the one case of healing, in the other of salutary fear.

RECITATION FOR THE DISMANTLING OF A HYDROGEN BOMB

From under the surface of the planet,
where we know, by statistics, you are waiting,
the White Trains sliding you through our emptiest spaces,
the small grassy doors to you trimly
sunk in the earth by desert or cornfield, then
the neat metal sheath, smaller than a mineshaft, with no
feeling of depth—
                  O how will you ever clearly
come to our sight? Surely our mortal hands
must take you, carry you, do, step by step, the terrible
laying you to sleep, or else— There is no third way.

We have seen you, as in the mirror of a shield,
suddenly standing tall on so many sides of us
like beautiful ghosts—able to hold completely
still on your columns of smoke, then making
a slight lateral tilt to take direction.
And then we realized—everything standing, the rattled
watch on the table a-tick—we were the ghosts,
and you, your power, our inheritors.

And turning from the shield, we saw the world
glare back, withholding: as if a nothingness

already lived in bird and twig, and they
turned their backs on us, to know it.
                                        But our minds
weren't ready yet; they could only wish and wish you
out of this world, out of ourselves.

    We might have thought of sending you
to wander, like a belled goat, the outer space
our fantasies wander so much now, caged
before the dreaming blips of our screen, inventing—
so we are told—a freedom untouched by you.
We would feel the endlessness you were shot into,
in which, if you destroyed,
past the range of our lenses, objects past our knowing,
it would come almost as a lightness, like the sense
of falling that comes before the fall of sleep.
It frees us without cheating you.

                                        For we
are grieved to give up a power—as if time
began to run backwards, our bodies shrank and dwindled
until they reached our mother's wombs, and disappeared.
Some days we'd even rather
use you, and use you up, than live the centuries
you won't quite vanish—the knowledge leaching through us
like your cores buried, after long debate,
in moon-polished canyonlands, always
a mile or so too near a major river . . .

The stars won't hide you. But there are precedents—
if analogy serves still—places
where things too big for us have been sung to sleep
once we knew we couldn't, or no longer wished to,
kill them.
            The flesh of death lay on the altar;
or a class where doctors (the one who speaks a woman,
soft-voiced) teach those in permanent pain to focus
on one word, and cross their legs in the right way,
as if singing, silently, to the thing in themselves . . .

My Lord, good night.

So we set ourselves with sorrow down, to sing to you,
sing you from the underground. First, of course, come
the treaties, the surveillance satellite cameras
pinpricking the globe—surface anesthesia
for our tireless fear of each other.

                      Then
it is like taking up hands
against some larger shape of ourselves—the skull-like shield,
the outer fissionable cortex, the inner
strange sky of the lighter-than-air . . . The self-destruct
systems (and the circuits that spoke to them, under the mountains);
the temperatures, equalled only
"in transient phenomena like exploding
supernovae."

                 My Lord, good night

                           —our arm
clad with the sun.

Go to sleep in us, as once, they say,
God went to sleep, and we trembled, not only that nothing
any longer overarched us, but that we
must contain what had.

             (The class is quiet. The doctors
come and go unnoticed, on their beeping
emergency calls. We have gone so far into
what hurts us, whether incalculable nervous twitch
or cancer. Time drifts outside us. Then the voice
—Look at something. Anything. Our eyes open wider
than seemed possible, through blear hospital panes, on things
a little different for each. Brown canyons
of bark. Light combed out past them. End of winter.)

EVENT HORIZON

(for Robert Pinsky, and to the memory of Louis-Ferdinand Celine—
imprisoned from 1945 to 1947, pending extradition on
charges of collaboration, in Vestre Faengsel in Copenhagen,
where a sentry did shout at him the opening line)

Hey you down there that takes it up the ass!
Ferdinand yells at me from his sentry tower
outside of it all now. Just what century

do you think you're in? *How We Became Posthuman?*
There's the Flat Stone Age, the Bone Age, the Age on its Knees,
the Age of Gunpowder—but I never mentioned

the age that sucked the universe up its tail . . .
Event Horizon! When do events stop happening?
When you've shown your waking up and your going to sleep

as well as your screwing, to everyone on your Webcam?
When the bombs no longer hurt the soldier's body,
he covers his ears with his hands, but in between

his brains have turned to jelly? Wear your wires
as if you wore your intestines on the outside,
you won't hear the train that's coming up behind you!

What's the UV forecast? What bridge collapsed, with no defect
but a hundred and forty thousand cars a day?
And don't you dare agree with me, you snotworm

who praised *soixante-huit*, then spent your whole life in school!
(And I'm him now, I'm the one below, who stumbles,
gaping through the prison chickenwire at the blue . . .)

Don't tell me they only let the ▇▇▇s and the ▇▇▇s
get angry in print now! I know it already! They blame
the cartoons not the rioters! not the old blind pig in the sky!

God is great! Blow up the Buddhas! Display the heads!
Blow up the Muslims too! Run your pipeline down from the Caspian!
Blood, music and lace . . . I'll show you the web of time. . . .

I don't know if your Vice President's secret phone call
meant he knew the attacks were coming, and I don't care . . .
Hide a needle in a haystack. Hide the fact

that matters among the million that might not. Shake up
the kaleidoscope all you like, it's the same shards, same dots
on your itsy-bitsy, teeny-weeny screens . . .

Oh the black weight never imagined, that sucks you under
when mind can't transmit any more . . . Yardbird, stumbling
with me in Vestre Faengsel, take your last gape at the blue

through the UV index—oh boy,
Priam, the Fates are gonna re-queer your ass!—
     [*Priami . . . quae fata, requiras*]
while the sentry crows! I never watched your damn screens,

Lili did, sometimes. The cheek of me, to have had That View,
the old Paris, like a fairy's wedding train,
before the bombings—the rooftops—red, black, soft gray—no wonder

they wanted to string me up from *le balcon*!

Laura Kasischke

Why Prose if It's a Poem?

I never set out to write a single poem in prose. In fact, I'd always avoided even *reading* those. They seemed to me to be cheating poetry out of its rightful music. Or requiring so much of prose it collapsed under the unfair burden of trying to sing with its mouth closed. When a prose poem worked (and I accidentally found myself reading many that did, fabulously), I didn't understand why or how. I thought maybe it was an anomaly, often brought on by having been originally composed in a language I didn't speak. I love line breaks, and the juggling act of choosing where to break a line, and I love the musical scoring that broken lines bring to the reading of poems. So why would I write a prose poem?

But, suddenly, I was writing nothing but prose poems. I also write fiction, but I never thought the writing of poetry in prose was a spillover from that completely unrelated act. I hope I'm not the only poet, or person, who is often completely baffled by her own decisions and behavior. I'm not sure I know why I went from dislike to infatuation with the prose poem (or so many other things in my life . . .) and then to love. Perhaps I could trace the initial burst of enthusiasm to some of the time I was spending with Paul Auster's wonderful anthology of French Symbolists. But, less impressively, I also think this came upon me while revising some of my nonprose poems (note the prejudice exposed in the language I've used here). I realized that what I was doing in many of those new poems (which have gone the way of the recycling bin) was using the line and its breaks to try to make my poems into songs. And we're not really talking major musical works here. We're talking pop songs. Kid songs. Corny songs. Hymns and carols accompanied by the banging of dusty pianos. Suddenly, reading those new poems so closely, the choices I had made—the line breaks, in this case, not the primordial rhythms and rhymes—made me cringe. I felt my line breaks took some fairly subtle (if I do say so myself) echoes and insinuations and led the reader through them by yanking, hard, on her arm and forcing her to drink.

Look! my line breaks said. I'm singing, I'm dancing, I'm rhyming my ass off!

Those poems didn't survive my experiment, which involved trying to stuff them into the prose-poem form like a corpse into a woodchipper. It turns out that, for me at least, a prose poem has to be conceived from the beginning as a prose poem. (And the other way around, too.) But I started to have what I considered some halfway successful experiments wherein I allowed the Mother Goose and open hymnal in me go full-tilt toward the kind of high rhyme and rhythm that originally drew me to the English language. I let my lower poetic instincts take over like a happy chorus of lovesick kids from the '50s, singing their hearts out while I buried them, deeply. As quickly as I could. I found they were still singing down there and that I loved that music. Precise and wild. Exuberant and stifled. There was a new liberation. Singing down there, they could sing louder. They *had* to sing louder. I called these poems my "Space, in Chains" poems, for reasons I hope are neither completely mysterious nor terribly obvious.

Of course, I was not the first in the line of a million prose poets. But I had the zeal of a convert. And by happy coincidence during this period of my maiden efforts, I came across this quote from Baudelaire:

> Which of us, in his moments of ambition, has not dreamed of a poetic prose . . . supple enough and rugged enough to adapt itself to the lyrical impulses of the soul.

And after that I had not only the ragged instinct and ambition for these experiments, but Baudelaire's endorsement to attach to my experiments, which are ongoing.

O, ELEGANT GIANT

And Jehovah. And Alzheimer. And a diamond of extraordinary size on the hand of a starving child. The quiet mob in a vacant lot. My father asleep in a chair in a warm corridor. While his boat, the Unsinkable, sits at the bottom of the ocean. While his boat, the Unsinkable, waits marooned on the shore. While his boat, the Unsinkable, sails on, and sails on.

MEMORY OF GRIEF

I remember a four-legged animal strolling through a fire. Poverty in a prom dress. A girl in a bed trying to tune the AM radio to the voices of the dead. A temple constructed out of cobwebs into which the responsibilities of my daily life were swept. Driving through a stop sign waving to the woman on the corner who looked on, horrified.

But I remember, too, the way,
loving everyone equally because each of us would die,
I walked among the crowds of them, wearing
my disguise.
And how, when it was over, I found myself
here again
with a small plastic basket on my arm, just

another impatient immortal
sighing and fidgeting in an unmoving line.

SPACE, IN CHAINS

Things that are beautiful, and die. Things that fall asleep in the afternoon, in sun. Things that laugh, then cover their mouths, ashamed of their teeth. A strong man pouring coffee into a cup. His hands shake, it spills. His wife falls to her knees when the telephone rings. *Hello? Goddamit, hello?*

Where is their child?

Hamster, tulips, love, gigantic squid. *To live.* I'm not endorsing it.

Any single, transcriptional event. The chromosomes of the roses. Flagella, cilia, all the filaments of touching, of feeling, of running your little hand hopelessly along the bricks.

Sky, stamped into flesh, bending over the sink to drink the *tour de force* of water.

It's all space, in chains—the chaos of birdsong after a rainstorm, the steam rising off the asphalt, a small boy in boots opening the back door, stepping out, and someone calling to him from the kitchen,

Sweetie, don't be gone too long.

RIDDLE

Mars, the moon, the man hammering on the roof all afternoon. The Greenwich clock, the worker bees, the agitated bubbles in a stream. They have a plan, these:

Theirs is the world of the railing nailed down around the canyon for the sight-seeing blind.

A woman sprawls out on a beach with a book, ready to read, but, opening it, she sighs. *Oh my.* She has settled down on her towel with the life story of a fruit fly—

Believable, chronological, but so quickly erased that it only serves to prove that the universe is made of curving, warping space. That, if you think about order, it becomes disorder. That to want to succeed is to fail: The way those satellites pointed at the stars pick up no sound at all, except, every few decades, the discordant music of a few chickens in a cave.

Oh, yes, oh, yes, I see.

There is a bridge from here to there. But we all know it is the kind of bridge that blows away. The kind of bridge made mostly of magazines, cheap beer, TV.

Not built to weather much at all.

Not war, nor despair, nor disease.

Not even health. Not even peace.

There is a chasm beneath it, and on one side my father is in his hospital gown watching that bridge blow around in the breeze—and, on the other side, waiting, is the mysterious unknowable thing that might have made him happy in this life:

What if it was me?

Carl Dennis

Point of View

Often when I look over poems that haven't worked out, especially poems that focus on other people, I find that the surest path to revision is tinkering with the point of view, experimenting with either narrowing the distance between poet and subject or stepping back. In such a case a few small changes, which take only minutes to make, can give life to what before seemed lifeless, impervious to all efforts at resuscitation. So I want to give an example here of one such revision, assuming that an approach that has worked for me might work for others as well.

The poem in question, "At the Wine Store," began as an attempt to dramatize the way a vocation can offer a perspective on the world. Here is the version that spent a good while in my "needs-work" drawer:

AT THE WINE STORE

This is a good bottle of wine,
One I can vouch for with certainty.
Not, to be sure, a miracle-worker
That can turn a day you hope to forget
Into one you hope to recall
Long afterward. Still,
If you're looking for something to serve
At a dinner welcoming home a friend
After an absence of many months,
This is the bottle for you.
Too good to drink by yourself
Unless you happen to feel so grateful
You need to lift a glass to your lucky stars.

A toast on the day you learn, after tests,
That the lingering pain in your side
Is nothing serious. A day to remember,
You'll say to yourself as you step
From the clinic into a street
That appears in your hour-long absence
To have been washed by a year-long rain
More cleansing than any rain before.
Drink this wine on that occasion
And you'll taste the sun and the earth
That gave of themselves to nurture it.
You'll lift your glass to the absent vintner
For his long hours of patient husbandry.
And why not a glass to those who raised him?
How easy to imagine his mother then
Treading the grapes as a barefoot girl
With her slender sisters in a giant tub.
They're all here in the first sip
From a bottle that in my opinion
Will serve as an instance as fine as any
Of how open you've always been
To the gifts the earth has offered,
How keen to enjoy them as they pass away.

This version of the poem, in which the owner of a wine store speaks to a "you," presumably the poet, has the strength proper to a dramatic monologue, the direct presentation of a character in the person's own voice, without the apparent mediation of the poet. The owner of the wine store offers here his judgment on the worth of a particular bottle of wine and, indirectly, on some of the sources of human happiness. When I tried to judge the worth of this version objectively, it seemed to me that though the details were vivid enough to make the speaker seem like a genuine individual, with a perspective that might be worth taking seriously, the poem as a whole was unconvincing. The main problem was that I could not imagine the poem actually being spoken in the implied dramatic situation. Would a wine seller be likely to make this statement to a customer, even if he believed all he said? Not if he was interested simply in promoting a bottle he liked as opposed to promoting a way of life. His judgment seems much too elaborate and presumptuous for the occasion, including advice on how to value friendship, how to handle concerns about illness, and how to enjoy life. Why all this instruction, unnecessary and unasked for? We seem meant to admire the speaker but wonder if we wouldn't find him, if we encountered him in the flesh, an intrusive bore. Such questions might lead the reader to the dark suspicion that the wine seller is only a thin mask for a poet with didactic designs.

When I set about revising the poem, I wanted to keep the details but make the rhetorical situation more credible, which turned out to involve leaving behind the dramatic monologue for a poem in which the speaker elaborates on what he takes to be the meaning behind the wine seller's laconic praise:

AT THE WINE STORE

He's a man whose words are few and measured,
The owner of the wine store at Hodge and Elmwood,
Who, when he pronounces a bottle "fine,"
Means neither that it's merely decent
Nor that it's so superb it can turn a day
One hopes to forget into a day
One hopes to recall long afterward.
He means if you're looking for something
To serve at a dinner welcoming home
A friend after an absence of many months,
This bottle won't disappoint you.
"Fine," implying the wine's too grand
To be drunk by yourself unless you're moved
To raise a glass to your lucky stars.
A toast, say, on the day you learn, after tests,
That the lingering pain in your side
Is nothing serious. A fine day,
You'll say to yourself as you step
From the clinic into a street
That appears in your hour-long absence
To have been washed by a yearlong rain
More cleansing than any you've known before.
In such a mood this bottle will prove so fitting
You'll raise a glass to the vintner's husbandry
And to whatever his parents did to encourage
His loyalty to the highest standards.
And why not a toast to the village women

You can imagine as barefoot girls
Treading the grapes in a giant tub?
They'll all be here in the first sip—
That's the unstated guarantee
Implied by the owner's terse endorsement.
A fine bottle that shows how open you are
To the gifts that sun and soil unite to offer,
How keen to enjoy them when they pass your way.

In this version, the owner of the wine store remains the central focus, but he is now a man of only one word, "fine," while the poet takes upon himself the task of spelling out the implications of the owner's pronouncement. Instead of a problematic dramatic utterance, we have the poet speaking to himself and perhaps to any "you" who might hear the owner's comment. The spelling out is elaborate and risks sounding somewhat too specific and too certain, but the reader is free to assume that the reading is based on some acquaintance, that the poet has had opportunity to ponder his subject's character. In rhetorical terms the poet is performing one of the traditional roles that poets are supposed to perform, stepping into the shoes of another, who for one reason or another remains overtly inarticulate. The great aesthetic danger for such a poem is to present a speaker who seems to be merely using the subject as an excuse for his own impressionistic associations, flaunting his fancy rather than trying to use his imagination to do the owner justice. To guard against this possibility, I worked to keep the voice of the speaker as objective as possible. He never appears overtly in the first person. His stance is consistently third-person limited, as he tries to enter into the owner's mind and to address the customers in the store as he surmises the owner might address them. If the poem works, the reader will be convinced that the speaker is not so much imposing his private thoughts on another but inviting another to speak through him.

Having argued that sometimes the most effective way to present a character is by resisting the pull of the dramatic monologue, I add here three poems in which that form is embraced for its directness and immediacy. The examples differ in the distance implied between the speaker and the poet.

LETTER FROM A SENIOR SECRETARY AT POTOMAC SCHOOL

I'd like to admit at the outset that the job we advertised
In American history might have been yours

If your application hadn't been misfiled,
As sometimes happened under our old procedures.
Under the new, I wouldn't have had to type
The letter sent you last month by the principal
To explain that our opening was already filled.
Then you wouldn't have made your angry phone call,
Which I hope you'll be relieved to know
I didn't mention to him. His cool tone
Wasn't meant to suggest indifference.
It's a tone our lawyers advise, to help us avoid
Conceding so much it leads to litigation,
A problem I'm not concerned with,
Being only three months away from retirement.
Here in this unofficial letter from me,
Which I'm asking you to keep confidential,
I want to point out that wherever you end up teaching
You'll have to learn how to deal with disappointment.
What will you do, say, when the textbook
Chosen by a committee in your new department
Turns out to be shallow as well as slipshod?
Will you look for another job, or will you
Use the occasion to show your students
How to spot the issues the book's neglected
And go looking elsewhere for enlightenment?
If I did my job by the book, I wouldn't have stayed
Late at the office this afternoon to write you this.
I'd have written you off as one of the self-absorbed
Caught up in avenging slights to his dignity.
Keep in mind I could be at home now,
Enjoying a taste for serious fiction and poetry
Passed on to me by my English teacher in high school,
Harriet Henderson. But here I am, extending myself
Beyond the call of duty. Now it's up to you
To ignore or appreciate my extra effort,
Just as the extra effort I hope you make
May or may not impress your students.
Even the best of them, remember,
May not be aware how much they're learning.
So you may not be aware how much these words,

Which now may seem addressed to someone
Dreamed up by me out of nothing,
May later seem to be meant for you.

ON THE BUS TO UTICA

Up to a year ago I'd have driven myself to Utica
As I've always done when visiting Aunt Jeannine.
But since last summer, and the bad experience in my car
With aliens, I prefer bus travel. Do you believe
In creatures more advanced than we are
Visiting now and then from elsewhere in the universe?
Neither did I till experience taught me otherwise.
It happened one night last fall after the Rotary meeting.
I'd lingered, as chapter chairman, to sort my notes,
So I wasn't surprised when I finally got to the lot
To find my car the only one there, though the shadows
Hovering over it should have been a tip-off
And the strong odor I had trouble placing—
Salty, ashy, metallic. My thoughts were elsewhere,
Reliving the vote at the meeting to help a restaurant
Take its first steps in a risky neighborhood.
So the element of surprise was theirs, the four of them,
Three who pulled me in when I opened the door
And one who drove us out past the town edge
To a cleared field where three-legged landing craft
Big as a moving van sat idling. In its blue-green light
I caught my first good look at their faces. Like ours,
But with eyes bigger and glossier, and foreheads bumpier
With bristles from the eyebrows up, the hair of hedgehogs.
No rudeness from them, no shouting or shoving.
Just quiet gestures signaling me to sit down
And keep calm as we rose in silence to the mother ship.
I remember the red lights of the docking platform,
A dark hall, a room with a gurney where it dawned on me
Just before I went under there would be no discussions,
No sharing of thoughts on the fate of the universe,
No messages to bring back to my fellow earthlings.

When I woke from the drug they'd dosed me with
I was back in the car, in the Rotary parking lot,
With a splitting headache and a feeling I'd been massaged
Hard for a week or two by giants. Now I feel fine
Though my outlook on life has altered. It rankles
To think that beings have reached us who are smugly certain
All they can learn from us is what we can learn
From dissecting sea worms or banding geese.
Let's hope their science is pure at least,
Not a probe for a colony in the Milky Way.
Do you think they've planted a bug inside me?
Is that why you're silent? Fear will do us more harm
Than they will. Be brave. Be open.
Tell me something you won't confide to your friends
Out of fear they may think you strange, eccentric.
If you're waiting for an audience that's more congenial,
More sensitive than the one that happens
To be sitting beside you now on this ramshackle bus,
I can sympathize. Once I waited too.
Now you can see I take what's offered.

PROGRESSIVE HEALTH

We here at Progressive Health would like to thank you
For being one of the generous few who've promised
To bequeath your vital organs to whoever needs them.

Now we'd like to give you the opportunity
To step out far in front of the other donors
By acting a little sooner than you expected,

Tomorrow, to be precise, the day you're scheduled
To come in for your yearly physical. Six patients
Are waiting this very minute in intensive care

Who will likely die before another liver
And spleen and pairs of lungs and kidneys
Match theirs as closely as yours do. Twenty years,

Maybe more, are left you, granted, but the gain
Of these patients might total more than a century.
To you, of course, one year of your life means more

Than six of theirs, but to no one else,
No one as concerned with the general welfare
As you've claimed to be. As for your poems—

The few you may have it in you to finish—
Even if we don't judge them by those you've written,
Even if we assume you finally stage a breakthrough,

It's doubtful they'll raise one Lazarus from a grave
Metaphoric or literal. But your body is guaranteed
To work six wonders. As for the gaps you'll leave

As an aging bachelor in the life of friends,
They'll close far sooner than the open wounds
Soon to be left in the hearts of husbands and wives,

Parents and children, by the death of the six
Who now are failing. Just imagine how grateful
They'll all be when they hear of your grand gesture.

Summer and winter they'll visit your grave, in shifts,
For as long as they live, and stoop to tend it,
And leave it adorned with flowers or holly wreaths,

While your friends, who are just as forgetful
As you are, just as liable to be distracted,
Will do no more than a makeshift job of upkeep.

If the people you'll see tomorrow packing the halls
Of our crowded facility don't move you enough,
They'll make you at least uneasy. No happy future

Is likely in store for a man like you whose conscience
Will ask him to certify every hour from now on
Six times as full as it was before, your work

Six times as strenuous, your walks in the woods
Six times as restorative as anyone else's.
Why be a drudge, staggering to the end of your life

Under this crushing burden when, with a single word,
You could be a god, one of the few gods
Who, when called on, really listens?

Mary Leader

Needlework Poems

```
[Aunt Consuelo's voice.^you are an ELIZABETH.^[WHICH]
[M[Now at five as I turn up the wick by the window]M]
[A[I see the lights moving at Sarah and Mary's. By]A]
[R[ §Susan Stewart of Philadelphia, Pen. in her §  ]R]
[I[poem     §      §      §      §      §      §      §   "The]Y]
[A[א   Factory Girls Get Up to Read Shakespeare"   ]?]
[N[  J§u§l§i§e§t§§L§a§v§i§n§i§a§§C§o§r§d§e§l§i§a  π]A]
[N[S W A N N A N O A   N O R T H   C A R O L I N A]U]
[E[--Dear Rebecca,          ~Ω~          Jan. 9, '89--]N]
[B[   Francine:navy-blue sweater, rose stripe.     ]T]
[O[~ Lucy:black Angora sweater, sky-blue beads.  ~]M]
[R[   Lee:blue denim shirt, rich burgundy  scarf.  ]A]
[U[~Eleanor W:burgundy/olive intricately knit.   ~]R]
[C[   Ann S:black sweater, skirt, tights, boots.  ]Y]
[H[~   Mary:I was there but what was I saying?  ~]?]
[S[   Probably the black-calico Skirt that Sara  ]T]
[G[~  gave me, or else "Old Blue"; brown  shoes  ~]A]
[R[   black tights, and either my Olive tunic or ]L]
[A[~∞~  my gray Turtle, both of whom love me.  ~∞~]L]
[N[E l l e n s  f i n e   W e   w i s h   y o u &]M]
[D[ j  ʹ    ʹ     ʹ     ʹ     ʹ    ʹ     ʹ     ʹ     ʹ     ʹ    f ]A]
[M[ a    xxx    Hello Juliana?          xxx      o ]R]
[A[ p     Î     Hello Augusta?          Î       r ]Y]
[S[ o           What are you doing tomorrow?     s ]S]
[B[ n xxx       Sleeping,                 xxx  y ]T]
[R[ i  Î             sleeping.          I     t ]E]
[O[ c  *     *     *     *     *     *     *     * h ]A]
[W[ a   **    **     **     **    **    ** ia ]R]
[N[By Eleanor Ross Taylor in her poem "New Girls."]N]
[C[   E.R.T.  b.Norwood N.C. Lives in Charlotte's-]S]
[H[ville, V i r g i n i a; also Ten. & Florida.    ]I]
[E[H e a t h e r   h a d   b e e n   w i t h   u s]K]
[C[ + ? + ¿ + ? + ¿ + ? + ¿ + ? + ¿ + ? + ¿ + ? + ]K]
[K+]   The whippoorwill is surer of her name     [?E]
[D++]   than we are sure of anything.          [??W]
[R+++]By- - - - - K a t h a r i n e - - - - -Jo[????]
[E++++]Haddox Privett  of  Pawnee Oklahoma  in [Eliz]
[S+++++] her poem "Watching My Daughter Sew" [Bishop]
[S]H U G  A N N  & M A R I A  4  M E    L O V E   ML[X]
```

FLAMESTITCH THROW (TO KNIT OR CROCHET)

```
D  D        D  D         D  D          D  D
AAAAAAA     AAAAAAAAA    AAAAAAAAA     AAAAAAA
NNNNNNN     NNNNNNNNN    NNNNNNNNN     NNNNNNN
 DDD DDD     DDD DDD DDD    DDD DDD DDD   DDD DDD
   A  AAAAAAA    A   AAAAAAA    A   AAAAAAA    A
        NNNNN          NNNNN          NNNNN
 D  D  DDD   D  D  DDD    D  D  DDD    D  D
AAAAAAA  A  AAAAAAAAA  A  AAAAAAAAA  A  AAAAAAA
NNNNNNN     NNNNNNNNN     NNNNNNNNN     NNNNNNN
 DDD DDD     DDD DDD DDD    DDD DDD DDD   DDD DDD
   A  AAAAAAA    A   AAAAAAA    A   AAAAAAA    A
        NNNNN          NNNNN          NNNNN
 D  D  DDD   D  D  DDD    D  D  DDD    D  D
AAAAAAA  A  AAAAAAAAA  A  AAAAAAAAA  A  AAAAAAA
NNNNNNN     NNNNNNNNN     NNNNNNNNN     NNNNNNN
 DDD DDD     DDD DDD DDD    DDD DDD DDD   DDD DDD
   A  AAAAAAA    A   AAAAAAA    A   AAAAAAA    A
        NNNNN          NNNNN          NNNNN
 D  D  DDD   D  D  DDD    D  D  DDD    D  D
AAAAAAA  A  AAAAAAAAA  A  AAAAAAAAA  A  AAAAAAA
NNNNNNN     NNNNNNNNN     NNNNNNNNN     NNNNNNN
 DDD DDD     DDD DDD DDD    DDD DDD DDD   DDD DDD
   A  AAAAAAA    A   AAAAAAA    A   AAAAAAA    A
        NNNNN          NNNNN          NNNNN
 D  D  DDD   D  D  DDD    D  D  DDD    D  D
AAAAAAA  A  AAAAAAAAA  A  AAAAAAAAA  A  AAAAAAA
NNNNNNN     NNNNNNNNN     NNNNNNNNN     NNNNNNN
 DDD DDD     DDD DDD DDD    DDD DDD DDD   DDD DDD
   A  AAAAAAA    A   AAAAAAA    A   AAAAAAA    A
        NNNNN          NNNNN          NNNNN
 D  D  DDD   D  D  DDD    D  D  DDD    D  D
AAAAAAA  A  AAAAAAAAA  A  AAAAAAAAA  A  AAAAAAA
NNNNNNN     NNNNNNNNN     NNNNNNNNN     NNNNNNN
 DDD DDD     DDD DDD DDD    DDD DDD DDD   DDD DDD
   A  AAAAAAA    A   AAAAAAA    A   AAAAAAA    A
 bride NNNNN   date   NNNNN  place  NNNNN   groom
 Andaluna DDD   May 15   DDD  Lafayette  DDD   Daniel
   Sirbu    A    1995     A   Indiana    A    Morris
```

> "All brought their distaffs, flax, spindles, standards,
> happles, and all the agoubilles useful in their art."

—*Les Evangiles des quenouilles*
[Gospels of the distaffs]
Anonymous, fifteenth century

My mother couldn't sew a lick
I *qua* daughter announced in a poem long after that mother

Was dead and buried in Highland Cemetery, Pawnee, Oklahoma.
Couldn't sew a lick. But that was a boast to her.

"I can't even sew on a button," she'd say at family gatherings
Right in front of the females stitching away: her mother-in-law,

Several nieces, her daughter, her sisters-in-law. . . .
Not her mother, although even Granny, no button-sewer-onner,

Was reputed to have tried knitting for the troops during WW II.
But (great-) Aunt Sara, childless, did a lot of needle-point in her day

And petit-point, and cross-stitch. Gatherings, holidays, the wives
And future wives in the living room with our distaffs, flax, spindles,

Standards, happles, and all the agoubilles useful in our art
While the men and boys watched football on television

In the den (somehow they knew exactly when to whoop and
Exactly when to groan, for they did both in unison).

She'd light another cigarette, repeat, "I can't even sew on
A button" (deep drag of smoke, inhaled, held, exhaled beautifully)

"I don't see how y'all can make all those little bitty stitches!"
Said in seeming admiration. My mother disdained needlework,

And for some very good reasons. It was the 1950s. What we girls,
Ladies, and women did with our distaffs flax spindles standards

Happles or agoubilles was not called "our art." Not remotely. It was
The 1960s, rural town. No "fabric arts" so-called. Needlework

Was no more "creative" than doing the dishes, and believe me,
Doing the dishes was not marveled at, whether mother

Washed and big sister dried or big sister washed and little sister
Dried or the housewife by herself. Needlework was *ipso facto*

Women's work; at best, "her hobby." And *my* mother's hobby was
Poetry. I'm typing up her poems. The document is now at p. 351.

It is due to her poem "Remains," about Aunt Sara, that I know
That when my mother's mother's mother made crab-apple jelly,

She "would place a geranium leaf / at the bottom of each glass
/ for the faint, exotic flavor that it gave." Bargain hunters out there,

You can now receive "Remains" in its entirety along with twenty
Other decent poems by logging on to and ordering:
    Author: Katherine H. Privett
    Title: The Dreams of Exiles
    Publisher: Holmgangers Press
    Date: 1981
    Our cost: $3

It was Katharine with an a- - - - - - - - - - - -Not Katherine with an e,
But what do Messrs. Barnes and Noble care?

Look, if you want the chapbook, send me a SASE and I'll mail it to you.
You can read "Watching My Daughter Sew" while sipping latte.

You can check out the back cover, see what my mother looked like.
She is wearing a beautiful heavy sterling silver medal. Or was

When our neighbor Ruby Lusk took the picture.
You can't tell from the blurry photo but the medal bore

The Sacred Heart on one side and the Blessed Virgin on the other.
My friend Arlene's mother was killed in a car-wreck when Arlene

Was six years old. Arlene—superb lawyer, by the way—remembers
An argument about whether her mother would be

Buried in her pearls ". . . cultured, of course, but they were *good*
Cultured pearls, and worth quite a bit."

Mimmy (Norwegian maternal grandmother in Saint Paul)
Felt that her daughter would *want* to be buried in her pearls.

Aunt Eleanor said "That's stupid. That's just stupid."
But Mimmy absolutely insisted, and Julie was wearing her pearls.

And Mimmy said, she always felt beautiful in those pearls. I always
Say "Arlene, you should write a short story, called 'Julie's Pearls.'"

Especially I enjoy using the scarcity of space to come up with abbreviations
and condensations, and likewise, I enjoy clear space, free to be left clear, in some
places, and in others, filled in with designs. In "Girls' Names," the tree motif, you
see, is there in the upper-case I's and the leaves of x's. The fact that the stitcher
(speaker) forgot to put in the circumflex on one of the I/trunks is just the kind
of mistake girls do make when attempting their samplers. I liked how place
names were often girls' names, and how mellifluous the names of Shakespeare's
heroines are, and how common words, like skirt, are sometimes a metonym for
a girl. Surely "Turtle" is a name for girls in some culture or other, and the way
the S fell into place before "hug" produced Shug, short for Sugar, which we girls
in Oklahoma were often called. Why not a girl named Swannanoa, Japonica,
Mother. I squeezed in little jokes as well—can you find the apple pie?—just as
I displayed serious intentions when evoking by icon both the means of writing
on a modern computer and the bitten apple from olden Genesis. Plus, the two
apple symbols are not entirely symmetrical in their placement.

In other words, with a sampler, or a quilt, or anything designed on a finite grid (including the typed or written or word-processed or typeset page), there are so many decisions to make and so many adjustments to make that you just can't have perfection. I love not only samplers and tapestries but also embroidered and appliquéd items for everyday use. Even apart from pictures, from needles threaded with rich or colorful threads, the actions of spinning and weaving, of knitting and crocheting and netting, and then of quilt-piecing, and of border-trimming, feel good to me, and *I want these actions to have expression in my poems.* I try to translate various forms of needlework into textile texts. "Flamestitch Throw" is one such. Some people would say it's "not a poem," I guess, but to me it shows you the following principles:

Needlework is democratic. Needlework is meditative, repetitive, and creative. It is historic. It lends itself to record keeping, particularly on the distaff side. It is mine; needlework is mine, and from long practice it is easy. It is lowly. When it claims to be poetry, it is rebellious. It is used to express love, to wish well, even to protect, magically, people one cares for. Japanese mothers of soldiers sew their sons special sashes to wear under their uniforms as an expression of the instinct to ward off harm. Not that it works. Not that the people in my poem, Anda and Dan, were able to avoid divorce court because I interconnected their names and commemorated their wedding with a verbal throw of flamestitch pattern. The point is not that one *can* protect those one loves, but that people will bring to bear *any* skill they have in *trying* to do so.

I often take needlework as my subject, too. Representing that branch here is a section from a new series called "Veillées." Now that I think about it, this series is a kind of latter-day "Girls' Names" for me. Here are Aunt Sara, Granny, Katharine (the same one represented in my first "Girls' Names" poem)—and how about naming a girl "Agoubille" or "Highland," "Lawyer" and/or "Heart"? Among us now are Ruby Lusk, Arlene, Aunt Eleanor, Mimmy, Julie. And Pearl. Like the daughter of Hester Prynne.

Eleanor Wilner

Process, After the Fact

The process I want to talk about is the one that goes on after the poem is written, when the poem's writer becomes its first reader. Since I believe that we write the poem we need to read, then it would seem that we are engaging something that we didn't yet know and may even have had strong reasons to avoid contemplating. This is often a longer process than the writing itself (though I am ignoring in that statement the years of thought, experience, and world that come together in the making of a poem), this coming to better understand a poem through a kind of intuitive, nonreductive cognition, one that meets the imagination on its own terms.

And this awareness of meaning that comes slowly, and only after the fact, does so because of the strange process by which a poem gets written. As we get out of the way and let the poem unfold and go its own way, the poetic imagination, which knows more than we do, produces a vision both revealed and re-veiled. This shapely, luminous veil is the language of metaphor, which protects and partly conceals what its resemblance reveals. It is the nature of symbolic action to enact meaning through images whose significance is neither single nor simple, nor available to us in a more conscious way until the poem is made and can become an object of reflection.

Surprised by where the poem below went as it gathered momentum, it was only much later, and spurred by someone's else's question, that I understood better not only what impelled the poem but what the poem had only alluded to through its figures. The poem began with a sound and not an intention; the title came after the poem was written, the dedication long after. The initiating sound was the terrible crying of an animal in pain—heard one childhood night on my grandfather's farm, an echo of what awakened again at a bullfight in Spain. The poem records only my own experience that day, until the last two stanzas when it moves from recall into imaginative invention. What, I wondered after the fact,

was going on there? Why the "bull with a man's head, knowing"? And why does
Ophelia appear, endowed as she is with fresh meaning?

ODE TO INNOCENCE

—to Victor Jara

What is that sound, like a foghorn but no sea near?

The night they put the ring in the bull's nose,
he bellowed in that low-down hollow way bulls have,
through the whole long dark and into the dreams
of the sleeping children, and next day, they
woke to a difference they couldn't find, as if
something had drowned in the night.

          Years later, Madrid. The gallant
young bull enters the ring, prancing, snorting,
lively as morning, confused a little by the shouting
crowd, and yet so confident, so trusting
of the force of his own health and the humans
who have provided, always, for his need—
sweet cows must be reward for this, and grass
at the end of it, an endless field of green.
That's when the picadors rode in. Huge men
on horses, carrying sticks with long metal spikes,
and they stuck him, and stuck him, martyred him   rhythm
like Sebastian, one thrust after another, till blood ran
from each carefully planted, each gaily decorated pick,
till it was hard to tell the ribbons tied on the picks
from the thin streams of blood pouring from each
of them, pain as decor on the flank.
And when he was tired, winded, beginning to
die, stumbling about the ring trying to escape
the pain to which he was pinned—
                          enter
the matador, all gold embroidered show, who,
in the last round of the bull's disgrace, waves
again and again, a huge cape in his face,

until the bull, flagging but furious, makes
a last feeble charge, seeing the red wash of blood
in his own failing eyes—now the matador
plunged in the sword, and slow, like an ancient
city toppling slowly into the sea when
the earth moved under it, the bull sank
to his knees, and gave his head a last shake
of something like disbelief, and died.

metaphors metaphors metaphors

If a bare hour in the pasture must suffice
for the long tunnel into the hot sun, and the crowd,
hungry, restless; if this was their pleasure—
what chance did she have, I ask you?
The ring was there waiting. The sound of doors
slamming. The echoing tread approaching
down a corridor of stone. The sound
of the crowd, its roar, and the bull,
the bull with a man's head, knowing.

minotaur

Better the pond than that,
                    better to go down singing, a bunch
of flowers perfuming the air, your last sight of earth
the sun in the leaves, and the blue sky turning . . .
while the court did what courts do, watched and did nothing,
reported back to the throne how it all went down:
the flowers, her smile, how slowly she sank,
and the singing. For, oh, she must have been mad,
what proved it to them was the singing.

court assumption misinterpretation

Now, why should Ophelia from *Hamlet* close a poem about the tormenting and killing of a fiery young bull for sport? She was an unplanned event, so the question was mine as well. In the play, Ophelia goes mad chiefly from the betrayal of a trusting naiveté. The queen describes with pathos Ophelia's drowning, how she fell into the brook, how she sang as her wide skirts slowly soaked and pulled her down—so it's clear, isn't it? That they must have watched as this was going on, and no one moved to save her. Her drowning had become another rapt spectacle at the death of innocence: as the poem says of the bullfight: "if this was their pleasure—what chance did she have, I ask you?" She was already entering the poem's field.

Still I wasn't sure why her death should seem so imperative, till much later when, queried by a reader, I became suddenly aware of the missing link, and its clue, the reference to a minotaur-like figure: "The sound / of the crowd, its roar, and the bull, / the bull with a man's head, knowing." For all at once I had remembered Victor Jara, the hidden key to the connection—maybe you know of him: he was a Chilean musician and poet, and he wrote the famous song of Allende's party, "*Venceremos.*" When Pinochet, with the CIA's collusion, staged the military coup that killed Allende and overthrew his democratically elected government, Jara was captured by Pinochet's thugs; with others, he was taken to the stadium where many were tortured and murdered. Jara's death is famous in Chile, because his torturers broke his hands and mocked him—"Now play your guitar"—but, it is reported, Jara went on singing and died singing, in what is now Santiago's *Estadio Victor Jara.*

Well, you know how the imagination works—how, as in dreams, it merges two figures into one where they share a meaning, but each adds something different to it—here it is the political man who is entering the arena to meet the bull's fate, knowing, as the bull did not, that he is going to be tortured and killed. So the meaning came fully home when I realized that Victor Jara, who died singing, and in an arena like the bull, was the connection to Ophelia, his fictional semblance, whose death was also a public display and who, like him, died singing. The bullfight in Spain had found its parallel in the arena of history.

And having unmasked its deeper subject, I dedicate it now to Victor Jara, so that the reader may know what had been informing this poem, but from below the conscious level, because it is most dreadful to remember such atrocity to our own kind, and I believe that poetry alludes in order to fend off graphic replication of the unspeakable, to refuse to reenact such desecration. Ophelia's singing already felt valiant to me before I knew its parallel in reality; she seemed not some mad woman drowning herself but a symbolic act of the lyric voice defying a lethal force, for in Denmark as in Chile a legitimate ruler had been murdered by a ruthless man who had taken his power—her fate a protective fiction, Jara's a literal fact. Of course, likeness is not identity—her figure is protective both as surrogate and as alternative to torture: "Better the pond than that." So this is the intricate knot that ties Ophelia to Jara and both to the fate of the young and spirited bull. And why, when a poem goes on well past its initial subject, it may take us beyond our intention to a place where meanings open and multiply.

I will offer one more poem that carries a masked allusion in the figure and its action but will leave it to you, the reader, to consider and read in your own way. It was a poem that seemed to happen before my eyes as I wrote, haunted by the words "the girl with bees in her hair," about which I knew nothing when I

began the poem. After it was written, I was still mystified. By closely observing
its details, I have been learning its meaning ever since—this girl from another
place, whose blank "unconcern" marks her not as a figure of intention but of
transport—call her messenger or metaphor. Perhaps connected to large public
events, as the poem's closing lines suggest, the figure comes, like Hamlet's ghost,
"in such a questionable shape" to invite questioning and to evade the canned
response normally invited by those events that, for ideological and political reasons, have been largely closed off from public discussion and serious contemplation.

THE GIRL WITH BEES IN HER HAIR

came in an envelope with no return address;
she was small, wore a wrinkled dress of figured
cotton, full from neck to ankles, with a button
of bone at the throat, a collar of torn lace.
She was standing before a monumental house—
on the scale you see in certain English films:
urns, curved drives, stone lions, and an entrance far
too vast for any home. She was not of that place,
for she had a foreign look, and tangled black hair,
and an ikon, heavy and strange, dangling from
an oversized chain around her neck, that looked
as if some tall adult had taken it from his,
and hung it there as a charm to keep her safe
from a world of infinite harm that soon
would take him far from her, and leave her
standing, as she stood now—barefoot, gazing
without expression into distance, away
from the grandeur of that house, its gravel
walks and sculpted gardens. She carried a basket
full of flames, but whether fire or flowers
with crimson petals shading toward a central gold,
was hard to say—though certainly, it burned,
and the light within it had nowhere else
to go, and so fed on itself, intensified its red
and burning glow, the only color in the scene.
The rest was done in grays, light and shadow
as they played along her dress, across her face,

and through her midnight hair, lively with bees.
At first they seemed just errant bits of shade,
until the humming grew too loud to be denied
as the bees flew in and out, as if choreographed
in a country dance between the fields of sun
and the black tangle of her hair.

                          Without warning
a window on one of the upper floors flew open—
wind had caught the casement, a silken length
of curtain filled like a billowing sail—the bees
began to stream out from her hair, straight
to the single opening in the high façade. Inside,
a moment later—the sound of screams.

The girl—who had through all of this seemed
unconcerned and blank—all at once looked up.
She shook her head, her mane of hair freed
of its burden of bees, and walked away,
out of the picture frame, far beyond
the confines of the envelope that brought her
image here—here, where the days grow longer
now, the air begins to warm, dread grows to
fear among us, and the bees swarm.

James Longenbach

A Romance with Information

THE IRON KEY

Mrs. Hunter is the only name I have for her,
A rich old woman who engaged my father, a painter,
To document her collection of keys.
Photographs she considered vulgar.

She lived in a mansard carriage house, painted black.
While my father made paintings of the keys
I made drawings of the house—
The Chinese parasol in a backlit case,
A sheikh's robe draped across the dining room table, under glass.

I added things that should have been there, a harpsichord.
I deleted what seemed mysteriously out of place.
Once, after I fell against my father's palette,
He had to scrub the paint from my hair.

Not to make things was idleness.
The house contained things to be made.
Not raw material: material that bore
Heavily the impression of having been used, worn,
Made previously into other things—

Like the house itself, once a place for horses,
Now the visible confirmation of what I knew by instinct
But had never seen: that only strange things could be beautiful.

McNamara, Westmoreland—outside the war was on.
Her house was where I lived in my mind.

For a time, I thought I'd be a painter too.
Then I thought perhaps a musician.
When I first saw San Simeone Piccolo
Floating across the Grand Canal,
I stepped into my mind.
I bought Mrs. Hunter a key.

MERCER STREET

Elizabeth, called Betty, took to her bed in 1952.
She had five daughters: Gale, Mary, Jean, Roberta, and Fran.
Geraniums in the window box, dahlias at the fence.
Albert lived three houses down.

Betty had a dog named Fuzzy, who roamed free.
At 5:00, when Fuzzy followed Albert home, she'd say
There goes a very smart man and a very smart dog.

Albert published the *General Theory of Relativity* in 1916.
After sleeping beneath the bed, refusing to eat,
Fuzzy limped in front of a moving car.
Time tells matter to move, matter tells time to curve.

Stewart, son of Fran, who lives at 1608,
Told me these stories, all of which are true.
To prove I liked solitude, which I didn't, never did,

I built my study in the basement when we moved to 1685.
Today, I see myself not as an older man
But as the man I might have been.
I wear his clothes, I look each morning to the sky.

Barberry, a locust chewing on a leaf.
Fran still drives downtown but once she gets
There can't remember why.

NIGHT FANTASIES

We slept above the Gargantuan Diner,
Second floor, Broadway and 111th Street.
We listened to a lot of records, we read a lot of books.
Brahms had not been dead for a hundred years.

All day I answered the phone at Fanwick and Rubin—
Fanwick and Rubin Dental Malpractice.
At night, when we opened the windows,
Exhaust blew in from the kitchen beneath us,
It covered our records with grease.

Once we bought wine with a bag of pennies,
Drank it on the island, traffic swirling past on either side.
Pollini playing Stockhausen,
Paul Jacobs playing Elliot Carter.
After the premiere of *Night Fantasies*

We walked across the park to the apartment.
You lowered the Venetian blinds,
Then pulled your jeans off
Purposefully, without shyness,
The fans of the Gargantuan rumbling below.
Augie's, the Mill, the sewer grate where you dropped your keys—

Carter turned one hundred on December 11, 2008,
Jacobs died of AIDS in 1983.
Of all the recordings of *Night Fantasies*

I like the one by Jacobs best;
It sounds like Schumann, flighty, lyrical.
It's out of print but you can listen to him playing
Busoni's transcription of Brahms' last work,
The organ chorale preludes, opus 122.
Arbiter Recordings, B0004W1KS.

SNOW

Snow that covers us from above,
Cover us more deeply.
Whiten the city with its houses and churches,
The red house and the yellow house,
The port with its ships.

Cover the Garden House
Where we could never get warm.
There was a fireplace so we learned to build fires.
We had a baby so we walked in the rain.

Cover the fields, cover the trees,
The river beneath us prodding its black stones,
The suffering of which I wasn't aware.

Cover the house where I grew up in New Jersey,
The basement where I learned how to paint,
To hammer a nail, to cut a silk screen.

The harpsichord I built,
The piano I played,
The attic where I stood alone in the cold
Listening for something, I didn't know what.

I hid a book in the eaves,
I couldn't find it when we moved.

Snow that covers us from above,
Cover us more deeply.
Cover the rooftops,
Cover the sea.

In January 2004, without having expected to do so, I returned to an apartment in Florence where I'd lived several years earlier. In the kitchen was a frying pan we'd bought, a vase we'd been given but left behind. In the drawer of a desk, in the back left corner, was a box of paperclips—my box of paperclips.

I felt as if I'd been dead, as if I'd returned as a ghost to inhabit the remnants of my life. And though I wanted immediately to write about this feeling,

I couldn't find a vocabulary. *I opened the drawer, and—lo—there was a box of paperclips!* I could describe the experience, but I couldn't make the discovery of those paperclips seem as otherworldly as it felt.

Only when I realized that words like *paperclips* were themselves the problem was I able to write a poem. I needed words like *clouds, mist, mountain*—words that could seem simultaneously mundane and otherworldly, words that could bring me to the concluding lines for the poem that I had in mind, a poem I'd call "Draft of a Letter."

> If you say the word death
> In heaven,
> Nobody understands.

"Draft of a Letter" became the title poem of my third collection; it generated an idiom—austere, hesitant, spooky—that carried me through the whole book.

But after *Draft of a Letter* was finished, I needed a new idiom if I was going to write any new poems.

> I wouldn't say this to everyone, but when I wrote
> *In heaven, if you say the word death, nobody understands,*
> I was thinking about paperclips.

These lines from "A Tenancy" did not happen because I made a conscious decision to use words like *paperclips* in a poem. I discovered the idiom for my most recent collection, *The Iron Key*, when I abandoned the short, heavily enjambed line of *Draft* for a line that was almost always syntactically complete, a line that demanded to be interesting as a rhythmic unit in itself, a line that asked to be filled with all the language I'd previously excluded—names, dates, addresses, receipts, catalog numbers.

> Elizabeth, called Bette, took to her bed in 1952.
> She had five daughters: Gale, Mary, Jean, Roberta, and Fran.

Working with this new line, I suddenly wanted to see how much ordinary information a poem could bear.

But a romance with information is a hedge against mortality, a way of imagining that we ourselves might be preserved: "To remember is to mourn, to forget is to be changed." This now seems to me the central theme of *The Iron Key*, but before I wrote the book, I couldn't have said it. To say it, I had to discover a new line.

C. Dale Young

The Necessary Fiction

COMPLAINT OF THE MEDICAL ILLUSTRATOR

Here is the incision,
it will be your gateway to the afterlife.
    Pull back the skin slowly.
The dead will tolerate only so much disturbance.

    The blood you believed
surrounded organs and muscle is not here, is it?
    See the liver,
it will bear you no fortune if eaten—

    the ancients lied.
The kidneys? No, they were ignored altogether.
    Now the thorax
is probably what you are most interested in—

    the lungs, the heart,
that all too popular organ among your profession.
    As you can see,
St. Valentine himself would not have liked it;

    it is not attractive.
Now tell me, poet: will this be enough
    to write your poem
about your artist, this Luca Signorelli?

Does *this*
really help you understand how or why
        he dissected
his only son's dead body?

INFLUENCE

Not even fever can conjure the stars
above Florence just before sunrise.
Yet we know that centuries ago it did,

or maybe it was the other way around.
Mrs. X, we were told, died
in severe respiratory distress.

The pathologist, our teacher (Mrs. X's
lungs in his hands), mumbled something
about the influence of the stars.

I will not attempt to imitate his accent.
He is from somewhere in Eastern Europe,
somewhere where they *really* like black bread,

even late in the evening before bed;
this, and more, he had mentioned before.
But Mrs. X, her lungs consolidated, dusky,

hemorrhagic, was our true lesson that day,
dare we forget the purpose of our studies.
Given a minor portion of her history,

a chance to examine her lungs thoroughly,
not one of us made the correct diagnosis.
And so, we were dismissed,

given one hour, a luxury we were told,
to ascertain the true cause of demise.
Seated at the microscope, we examined,

one after another, Mrs X's slides, each
of us noting the classic cytoplasmic inclusions,
the overwhelming inflammation.

Only then did we understand what our teacher
understood long before looking under a microscope—
Influenza: under the gravest influence of the stars.

TORN

There was the knife and the broken syringe
then the needle in my hand, the Tru-Cut
followed by the night-blue suture.

The wall behind registration listed a man
with his face open. Through the glass doors,
I saw the sky going blue to black as it had

24 hours earlier when I last stood there gazing off
into space, into the nothingness of that town.
Bat to the head. Knife to the face. They tore

down the boy in an alleyway, the broken syringe
skittering across the sidewalk. No concussion.
But the face torn open, the blood congealed

and crusted along his cheek. *Stitch up the faggot
in bed 6* is all the ER doctor had said.
Queasy from the lack of sleep, I steadied

my hands as best as I could after cleaning up
the dried blood. There was the needle
and the night-blue suture trailing behind it.

There was the flesh torn and the skin open.
I sat there and threw stitch after stitch
trying to put him back together again.

When the tears ran down his face,
I prayed it was a result of my work
and not the work of the men in the alley.

Even though I knew there were others to be seen,
I sat there and slowly threw each stitch.
There were always others to be seen. There was

always the bat and the knife. I said nothing,
and the tears kept welling in his eyes.
And even though I was told to be "quick and dirty,"

told to spend less than 20 minutes, I sat there
for over an hour closing the wound so that each edge
met its opposing match. I wanted him

to be beautiful again. Stitch up the faggot in bed 6.
Each suture thrown reminded me I would never be safe
in that town. There would always be the bat

and the knife, always a fool willing to tear me open
to see the dirty faggot inside. And when they
came in drunk or high with their own wounds,

when they bragged about their scuffles with the knife
and that other world of men, I sat there and sutured.
I sat there like an old woman and sewed them up.

Stitch after stitch, the slender exactness of my fingers
attempted perfection. I sat there and sewed them up.

THE HANGED MAN

I know a lot about the second cervical vertebra.
And because I love precision and accuracy, I refer
to it as the axis, the name buried in the Latin,
meaning *chariot*, meaning *axle*, meaning the line
around which something revolves or turns.

How is that for being exact? And to break the axis,
to fracture it, is rare. A neurosurgeon will tell you
it comprises only 15% of cervical spine injuries.
Although we live in the 21st Century and one
would assume a more clinical name for breaking

the axis, such a break is still called the Hangman's
Fracture. I need not explain the derivation
of such a name. Not divers or thrill-seekers,
but heretics and those charged with treason
provided such a term—the hanged man, the monster,

the witch and the unloved. Go ahead; break the bone.
Shatter it. Leave the cracks to be seen on an x-ray.
The hanged man walking tilts his head to the side
opposite the cracks. He tilts his head away from
such an insult. He tries to appear normal.

But there is no name for such behavior, no clinical
name to describe this odd activity of avoidance.
I have spent years studying avoidance. I am
an expert now. I never say the hip bone is connected
to the leg bone. I say acetabulum, say head of the femur.

The editors of this anthology asked each poet to include a page or two dis-
cussing the process behind the works selected. At first, this request seemed
simple, but it became, for me, the most difficult aspect of this project. And so I
put it off, decided instead to focus on the poems. "Complaint of the Medical Illustrator" was first drafted in 1990, before I entered graduate school for creative
writing and before I entered medical school. "Influence" was drafted in 1998, in
the year after completing medical school. "Torn" was drafted in 2003, a year after
finishing my residency, and "The Hanged Man" in 2010. Strangely, I have poems
here that span twenty years of writing.

What surprises me most? The poems don't seem as if they were written over
a twenty-year period of time. I am a poet who is always convinced he is doing
something new, and yet, and yet, as time passes I realize these ideas of the radical new are fictions. I suspect now looking at these four poems that I need to
believe that I am doing something new in order to get the draft of the poem

down. But just as one cannot overnight become a new person, I suspect it is similar with writing poems. One cannot completely be reborn every few years as a writer.

If there is one thing I have learned in this venture, it is something my friend Rick Barot said to me years ago: "Every poem conjures a specific moment and time for a poet." He was speaking about his own work, but I see now it applies to me as well. I have always distrusted the confessional mode of contemporary poetry, and yet I am fascinated by the power of connection between the speakers of such poems and their readers. I realize that I have spent my life so far as a poet trying to capture that relationship between speaker and reader without actually being confessional, without actually relaying my own life directly. Trust me, I am not naïve enough to believe that my life isn't here in these poems, but my real life isn't here for a reader the way it is in a memoir: the poems are not autobiographical in that way. But, that said, as Barot once said to me, each poem is a record of a particular point in my life, even if indirectly.

One cannot escape one's life, even if that escape is often what prompted many of us to write in the first place. As a physician, it fascinates me how medicine enters my work, even in a poem written before I ever attended medical school! I have confessed nothing, and yet I am completely here in these poems. In the end, I hear my own mind cogitating in these poems. And this is satisfying to me because that is what drew me to poetry in the first place, that chance, that odd opportunity to hear and witness another person's mind at work, at play.

Alan Shapiro

Public Places, Night

GAS STATION REST ROOM

The present tense
is the body's past tense
here; hence
the ghost sludge of hands
on the now gray strip
of towel hanging limp
from the jammed dispenser;
hence the mirror
squinting through grime
at grime, and the worn-
to-a-sliver of soiled soap
on the soiled sink.
The streaked bowl,
the sticky toilet seat, air
claustral with stink—
all residues and traces
of the ancestral
spirit of body free
of spirit—hence,
behind the station,
at the back end of the store,
hidden away
and dimly lit
this cramped and
solitary carnival

inversion—Paul
becoming Saul
becoming scents
anonymous
and animal; hence,
over the insides
of the lockless stall
the cave-like
scribblings and glyphs
declaring unto all
who come to it
in time:"heaven
is here at hand
and dark, and hell
is odorless; hell
is bright and clean."

CAR DEALERSHIP AT 3 AM

Over the lot a sodium aura
within which
above the new cars sprays
of denser many colored brightnesses
are rising and falling in a time lapse
of a luminous and ghostly
garden forever flourishing
up out of its own decay.

The cars, meanwhile, modest as angels
or like angelic
hoplites, are arrayed
in rows, obedient to orders
they bear no trace of,
their bodies taintless, at attention,
serving the sheen they bear,
the glittering they are,
the sourceless dazzle
that the show case window

that the show room floor
weeps for
when it isn't there—

like patent leather, even the black wheels shine.

Here is the intense
amnesia of the just now
at last no longer longing
in a flowering of lights
beyond which
one by one, haphazardly
the dented, the rusted through,
metallic Eves and Adams
hurry past, as if ashamed,
their dull beams averted,
low in the historical dark they disappear into.

SUPERMARKET

The one cashier is dozing—
head nodding, slack mouth open,
above the cover girl spread out before her on the counter
smiling up
with indiscriminate forgiveness
and compassion for everyone
who isn't her.

Only the edge
is visible of the tightly spooled
white miles
of what is soon
to be the torn off
inch by inch receipts,
and the beam of green light in the black glass
of the self scanner
drifts free in the space that is the sum
of the cost of all the items that tonight
won't cross its path.

Registers of feeling too precise
too intricate to feel
except in the disintegrating
traces of a dream—
panopticon of cameras
cutting in timed procession
from aisle to aisle
to aisle on the overhead screens
above the carts asleep inside each other—
above the darkened
service desk, the pharmacy, the nursery,
so everywhere inside the store
is everywhere at once
no matter where—
eternal reruns
of stray wisps of steam
that rise
from the brightly frozen,
of the canned goods and food stuffs
stacked in columns onto columns
under columns pushed together
into walls of shelves
of aisles all celestially effacing
any trace
of bodies that have picked
packed unpacked and placed
them just so
so as to draw bodies to the
pyramid of plums,
the ziggurats
of apples and peaches and
in the bins the nearly infinite
gradations and degrees of greens
misted and sparkling.

A paradise of absence,
the dreamed of freed
from the dreamer, bodiless
quenchings and consummations
that tomorrow will draw the dreamer

the way it draws the night tonight
to press the giant black moth
of itself against the windows
of fluorescent blazing.

After *Old War*, my most recent book, which like most of my books contains
plenty of poems based on personal experience, I decided to write a book without narrative or direct personal experience of any kind. I wanted to write a book
about public life, the public structures within which and by means of which
we embody and enact our identities as members of a culture or society. These
three poems are from a long series of poems entitled "Night of the Republic."
All the poems in the sequence are set in public places *at night* when no people
are in them. The public places range all over the social, commercial, and political spectrum, everywhere from a gas station restroom or car dealership to a
supermarket, convention center, or church. In imagery that is meant to be both
surreal and familiar, the poems try to evoke the private desires, obsessions, and
forms of power implicit in the public structures that comprise our social lives.
They explore the strangeness of the public sphere, a sphere that's weirdly everywhere and nowhere, empty and crowded. The challenge of the project was how
to find a variety of ways of inhabiting emptiness, how to suggest or hint at the
dense human often ugly political realities behind spaces that are often (at night
anyway) very beautiful. I wrote all the poems in long sentences moving through
short free-verse lines. The prosody I hope catches the sensation of the imagination in the presence of familiar things made suddenly strange; the syntax turning from line to line is trying to embody or enact the vision of a public place
as it turns in imagination from day to night, from civic identity to the private
irrational desires that identity both accommodates and disguises.

Daniel Tobin

The Reaches

THE JETTY

      reaches, a stone sentence, across the bay—

its jigsaw syntax entered like hopscotch
from Land's End,
                entered the way wrens
step, step on sidewalks, crushed shells,
looking for seed,
            as if unsure of earth,

until it feels natural to be outside
the known scope,
             and you follow
the jumbled puzzle out farther

than you first expected, toehold
by toehold,

       to where the broader slabs
give certain footing, a way over water,

Appian, you think, miraculous
the way it seems to float
                on tidal flats,
beach-grass wavery as prairie
sprouting from wavelets, tinselate,

the whole horizon threatening to blend
earth, sky and sea,
              though sea, sky, and earth

stand poised, pristinely, on the glinting
edge,
      so you come to feel yourself
suspended in a fluency that would be

ethereal if not for the *thump, thump*
of a festival drumming intermittently

from the town, over parabolic sands,
like finest brushstrokes lacing the shoals—

shallows of moon-snails, welks, skate-eggs,
these currents like sandcoils redoubling

in pools where shucked pilings, scarified
granite,
              brace to colonies of rockweed
that flail in sediment's plangent ooze,

the soft siphons of lowlier lives
shooting invisibly from under,

trumpet worms, dogwinkles, bits
of swamp-pink and poverty grass

awash in foam the color of meringue,
salt spray rust in the tide's
                            recursive flow,
a slow parting-of-the-waters revealing

articulations of tablets into shifting
dunes that have arranged themselves

into just this measure, as if to say
Nothing needs you here—
                        not the sundews

and sanderlings, plovers, hovering gulls;

not even the lighthouse at Long Point,
a beacon at the brink of the human—

you are an earthstar tumbling its spores
into the living waste,
                    the risen pleroma,

your name a net caught in the hollow
between stones
                  while the tide sounds
the length of this transit, susurrant

fountain, a summoning from under,
and all of it gone by evening.

THAT IS TO SAY

In memory of Nathan A. Scott, Jr. (1925–2006)

Fall, and the terraced ascensions of this Lawn
Buzz with the callow treasons of its clerks,
       And along the colonnade
The sun makes a gnomon of each column and brick
Where light waves congregate astride their opposite
       On every wire-edge of shade.

From above, the Rotunda's unblinking eye
Looks up, looks back as though from where it came,
       Some archetype or figure,
And not a built thing imagined into presence
By faulty, human genius on the backs of slaves—
       A wound that would nurse its cure.

From higher still, let's say a satellite map,
With every turning threshold of range and scope
       The center grows center-less,

An assemblage of "dreamy anonymity,"
Strangely depthless, a flat and fracturing collage
          Of small lives moving en masse

Like passing circuits across a motherboard
No matter their ambitions or pains, no matter
          But matter animated
By what you called the frailest "fragments of adjustment"
Our idea of the world a frontier in extremis,
          Derelict, desolate,

Which is to say, as you would say, what you saw
As a fall and a forgetting, a banal eclipse
          That leaves us in the meantime,
An erased horizon, and earth unchained from its sun.
What good, then, apropos of nothing, to savor
          The fine meal, the martini,

The chatty communion of friends at home,
The calling of others to learn otherwise?
          I only want you to see,
The great saint wrote, which was the creed you lived by
And what you taught, a way of making poetry
          A way of letting-be,

Until the part could somehow cicatrize the whole,
The cheap synecdoche like an empty sequined glove
          Become a bright beholding.
As in Bearden's *The Return of the Prodigal Son*
Where the one who's come back looks stanched in gauze,
          Humbled, raw, his enfolding

Waiting in the advent of those who greet him,
Themselves radiantly particulate
          With scraps, bits—surfaces
The artist improvised on this kaleidoscopic frame,
Where the one who's escaped the sty's stench and mire
          Turns outward from the faces

Of those who will embrace him, of those he will embrace,
Toward us as toward a lens, his chest shining
      With its breastplate of shook foil,
The cast-off bottle that bound him secured in rope,
His two horizons behind—the ashen and the risen—
      And that candle at the fulcrum

Under the figure's wide, iconic eye, burning
As in a tabernacle, so you would have us see
      Each such meeting together
As a ritual of color, depth of field, the promise
Of an imminent All-in-All that flashes instantly
      In every instant's shutter.

That is to say, as you would say, everything
Is threshold, and is so by way of being
      Providently on the way,
Itself and not another thing, and so the advent
Of a coming home: It is the slug's slim prayer
      That teaches how to pray,

Riding its losses across a patch of ground,
Till one believes with each leaving in the kinship
      Of things that do not look akin,
The circle squared in a turn of the scope. That is to say,
We are gathered wherever we go by way of love,
      And nothing will be forsaken.

LATE BLOOMER

Something whispered I wanted more of myself.
That's how I turned into the *fleur* of myself.

The lake. The ripple's shimmer. That lilting face.
I'll guzzle the infinite pour of myself.

What is this flow I feel, its course through soft bone?
The current? The mother load? The ore of myself?

Fill me with all things. Empty me completely.
I winnow and still am the store of myself.

Imagine earth, the stars—all space expanding—
And finding everywhere the core of myself.

If soul's estate means a mansion's many rooms
Then someday I will take a tour of myself.

Do you think me insane, my hypocrite twin?
A catatonic's stare? The whore of myself?

Call me this. Call me that. Call me what you will.
I surpass beyond words the lore of myself.

Time blooms with space, and their sum's all I am.
I am forever the before of myself.

Beauty is Truth, Truth Beauty, Beauty is Truth . . .
X to nth power is the shore of myself.

Narcissus—the name a wind passing through wind.
Now watch me step through the door of myself.

When physicists want to picture the structure of reality—three dimensions of space plus one of time—in the expanding universe we inhabit they often turn to the dubiously simple image of a balloon inflating from an infinitely dense point called a singularity. As the balloon expands every point recedes from all the others, which is why the stars and galaxies are red-shifting at this moment away from our points of view, just as we are receding from the perspectives of anyone who might be watching, hypothetically, from any one of a "gazillion" vantages (to suggest the unimaginable with an appropriately childish word). Of course, all the data imply the universe is accelerating in its expansion in ever-more-rapid fast-forward. It's hard to get the full implication of an evolving universe from an inflating balloon, the most curious component of which is the presence of consciousness itself, whatever that is, really, in the context of a universe or, for that matter, a multiverse.

A poet, by sleight of thought, might ask how such a vibrantly complex intuition about the nature of dynamical structure bears on the decidedly local confines of verse-making. What does a line, stanza, inherited form, or instance of free verse have to do with so elusive a conception of structure? Think of a dark-matter particle, this second, passing like a diamond bullet unnoticed through your forehead. Or, rather, think of the page as Flatland where the poem resides in its two dimensions, but latent with the poet's investment of meaningful amplitude. Enter the attentive reader/listener, and the poem lifts again into a higher dimension of existing, no longer exclusively on the page but in the mind's individuated time. It is not an arbitrary lift-off, but one guided by the spatial and temporal orchestrations the poet has made, a realization accomplished both by accident of experience and by the labors of intuition and deliberative choice.

My own poem, "The Jetty," found its incipient structure early on when I recognized that it needed to move from title to final word—the poem in its entirety— as a single sentence: "The Jetty // reaches. . . ." The challenge, of course, is how to keep the sentence evolving both grammatically within the laws of language's "physics" and evocatively through a series of unfolding clauses that could at once track the world perceived and the mind perceiving the world and naming it. Of course, I considered nothing so much at the time. I wanted to get the details and get them in the right order with the right pacing, music, arc of recognition—a physical embodiment of the jetty on the page; which is why the poem's slippage of lines moves as a two-dimensional allusion to the jetty itself while the poem's pacing gains support through the substructure of a loose iambic verse.

The poem "That Is To Say" works somewhat differently with structure in that it assumes the template of an Auden-like attraction to fixed form and seeks to create internal pressure, both emotional and speculative, within the self-evident edifice of its strictly rhymed stanza. My own first inclination is often architectural, and the challenge is to give each part and moment of the poem its vitality within the whole. The poem channels some of the language and tonalities of my teacher, the theologian and literary scholar Nathan A Scott Jr. The poem gets its title from a phrase he used repeatedly in his speech and in his writing, and iterations of the phrase repeat throughout the poem as an echo device, a way of honoring and conjuring beyond the merely elegiac. Like "The Jetty," "That Is To Say" uses long sentences expressively and inquiringly. The challenge of weaving sentences across long lines, clause by clause, through the complex grid of structure, is most strongly present for me in this poem in the three and a half rhymed and off-rhymed stanzas that describe Romare Bearden's great painting *The Prodigal Son*. Among other things the poems share a fascination with "the kinship / of things that do not look akin," and while differently structured, both poems seek to embody similar habitations of thought and feeling, similar vantages on reality.

Finally, "Late Bloomer" uses the structurally curtailing couplet of the ghazal to unlock associatively an expansion of the Narcissus myth through a reversal that shifts the grid of inherited story from static self-containment to a progressive and one might say eternal embrace of the self outward in relation to all that the self is not—"All goes onward and outward, nothing collapses." Such is Walt's *Welt* hidden in Narcissus's Self-Song. The expanding Narcissus, the ever-exfoliating bloom of all that is . . . Dr. Johnson warned poets not to count the stripes of the tulip, and Coleridge privileged the *naturans* over the *naturata*, the dynamical structure of reality over the occasional. The poem, of course, should ideally fuse vital structure with the poet's nominal perception in every aspect of its composition. That is when the fleeting reality we inhabit crystallizes into presence both in the ear and on the page. That is when—that is to say—structure becomes incarnate as form.

Brooks Haxton

Five Versions

"Looking Up Past Midnight into the Spin of the Catalpa Blossoms" is the first poem in my most recent collection, *They Lift Their Wings to Cry*. I was thinking that I wrote it quickly. But I find in my computer files that I spent twelve hours and fourteen minutes writing about twenty drafts over the course of six months. The first version surfaces in a series of poems and notes for poems generated in mid-June a few years ago, none of the rest of which I kept. That draft probably came before the catalpa in my back yard, a spectacular tree, fully flowered. In the second version, I described falling catalpa blossoms, as an effect of gravity, which had something to do with the magnetic field, and with the core of the earth, and the thoughts in the core of the brain. After a few more drafts I was associating the petals of a flower with the whorled shapes of magnetic waves, and gravitational fields, and burgeoning thoughts. The idea that the narrator might be looking up and making these tenuous analogies because he's lying in his front yard drunk was the last big change that came to me. After that, I did a little tinkering, and the poem was finished. These five drafts include one of the earliest, three intermediate, and the published versions.

06-16-06

The earth's magnetic field
is simpler than the mind,
but no more pure. Pure
consciousness, they say,
is conscious only of itself.
The idea of an acorn
is impure, according to this
rule. The image of an underwater

spring at night keeps flowing
in the darkness just behind
my eyelids where the shadows
of the sycamore leaves flicker.

MAGNETIC FIELD AT SOLSTICE

After the long heat of an afternoon
with hundreds of catalpa blossoms
falling through the musk of summer
petals opened from the spinning
molten core of Earth
toward Jupiter, the brightest dot
just now among the stars. Pure
consciousness, they say,
dwells only in itself.
While moths slammed
head first into the porch light,
underwater springs
kept flowing far down
somewhere in my sleep.

SOLSTICE

from molten iron
inside the earth
concentric whorls
of a magnetic field
unfold
under the solar wind.

consciousness
turns inward

moths slam head first
into a light bulb

hundreds of catalpa blossoms
pour musk into the calm night
disattach and fall

while springs flow
underwater in my sleep

SOLSTICE

From molten iron inside the earth
concentric whorls of a magnetic field
unspool, bending, under the solar wind.
Consciousness turns inward. Moths
slam head first into a light bulb.
Hundreds of catalpa blossoms
pour musk into the calm night,
disattach, and fall. Springs
flow underwater in my sleep.

LOOKING UP PAST MIDNIGHT INTO
THE SPIN OF THE CATALPA BLOSSOMS

I came home drunk without my key
and lay down in the yard to think.
Inside my skull on damp grass thoughts
spun inward. Whorls of a magnetic field
exfoliated under the solar wind,
so that the Northern Lights above me
trembled. No: that was the porch light
blurred by tears. Moths slammed
head first into the light bulb. Maybe
they need bigger brains. Me too.
I closed my blurry eyes, and springs
flowed underwater in my sleep.

Heather McHugh

Writing as an Act of Reading

In social settings I can go with the flow, generally, but when I'm by myself I'm as reflexively contrarian as any other two-eared double-hung human being. Thus for a time I took reading and writing for terms of contrast, or even mutually exclusive acts.

But now I see them (like most counterpoises) as aspects of a single entity. All literary reading is reflective, as it puts things together, becomes (in etymological exactitude) compositional; and all literary writing, done by selective delectation, is a species of reading.

A reader has a signature. It's shaped not only in the choice of texts he makes from among others. (The history of someone's bedside book pile is his moving portrait-through-time.) His signature is also there in the graph of his attentions through a single text—the direction and intensity and speed of the attention he pays as he navigates the literary matter. To translate a passage is to become especially aware of the flows not only from one language to another but within a single language; is to be vested with a sense of the craft with its tiller and net—a heavy sense of readerly responsibility for the cull and character of your *atten-tions* (even though you had started the translatorial task by feeling relieved of your *intentions*). You shape what you are shaped by. You shape what you take in and what you give out. As with breathing, there are *so* two ways about it.

Look at *legere*—the root of selection, election, intelligence, religion, legality. Its oldest sense is a split (thus doubled) one. The Latin infinitive means to gather or collect but also to choose or pick out. If you go back etymologically you find it's related to *lignum*, or firewood—something you selected and collected (not necessarily in that order) and incidentally, I'd add, something you'd use for heat.

In most languages the word for reading derives from this *legere*, though in Eng-lish we tilted toward a word related (via the sense of interpretation) to *riddle*. (Gotta love that.)

Read is conjectured to have derived from an Indo-European root involving reason and counting. But *legere* has its ledgers and the occasional etymological emphasis on enumeration too. Donne called poetry "the art of numbers." For anyone with a heartbeat, there's no fundamental antithesis between the metrical sciences and the metrical arts. What really counts, if you ask me, is the degree to which assortment and assembly can contrast as they conspire. Great collectors are simultaneously great selectors: despite their prefixes' contrariness, the two are not at odds. Things picked out are put together. Things gathered are sorted.

I like the etymological fidelity of a word like *composition* when it applies in par-ticular to work whose elements I most literally "put together," assembling them from item lists in existing reference texts. The "putting together" is what syn-tactifies the new ensemble. This modus operandi is, I think, a special instance of the general case of art. From the pool of things you choose items; arranging items, you suggest relationships.

Hence my choice of poems here. Even when it's putatively arbitrary, the choice of field from which you gather your materials, the quasi-physical sources of the matter of your art, confesses something about you, the artist. Thus, I believe, my love of lexicons tells something about poets, who so materially love the words they enlist. They love the choirs and quirks of words; plunder the choir to quicken the quirk; and live by the means of the verbal matter, the downright word-working fuel of it all.

As for any incidental blurring of the boundaries between means and meaning, syntax and semantics, numbers and letters, writer and reader, intimation and ultimation—yay! So much the worse for any Manichaean meanies out there! And so much the merrier for verse!

Of the source material for the older of these two poems I no longer remember the bibliographic specifics—it was a battered old paperback, an etymological dictionary, something passing briefly through my hands, from which I hooked a few oddball fish on lines, and some of whose entries, I would soon be informed, were now considered "unreliable." Such information is of (certain) interest—but the authority of scholarly fact is not, in fact, the poem's business. (When the gods hate a man with uncommon abhorrence, said Seneca, they drive him into the profession of a schoolmaster.) The poem engages in a sort of networker's pleasure, making its cat's cradle using the oddest threads it could find, in the spool-rooms of yammer and yarn.

The selecting out, and rearrangement, of attractively interactive oddities is constitutive of art. The visual artist twigs something from the forest; the musician plucks something from the Sound. From the litter of the littoral, one lifts a shell; one's skull is prompt to resonate. Pressing an odd noggin to the odd nautilus, one soon enough reflects on men in moons or finds oneself singing of Nod, to Nadie . . . Such is attention's capacity for traverse: one moment a dunghill, the next a universe.

I've always been drawn to scrappish little numbers in nonliterary settings: the texts on discarded cereal boxes; fortunes on bubble gum wrappers; warnings in hotel lobbies (notably the one I saw in LA: "in earthquakes this elevator may fall uncontrollably"); directives in airports (because strictly speaking, oh students of literature at the TSA, the suspect must never be the one who's suspicious—you do not desire him to be so; in general, an unsuspecting suspect is the best. But *us* you wish to be suspicious; by laws of land and language, what your placard ["Report suspicious activity"] means is that we must report ourselves. Thus, alas, is language implicated in the law. Life has its own ludic way with logos now. Legos have logos.)

Myself, I'm not at liberty to overlook such less-than-licit readerly delights. Did you know, by the way, the word *delight* derives from *delicere*—to entice or lure (as if toward sin)? Only by some slippage did its spelling change from the venerably correct (if shadier) *delite*—to arrive at *delight*—via a false association between the second syllables' homophones. As a selector/collector, as a writer/reader, I cull from the stream of all language such peculiarities and pleasures, shapes enticing (even arresting) to eye and ear and intellect, and wind up delving far too frequently, delinquently, into the delectative.

QED.

Where was I? In the thick of essayistic things. The second set of borrowings was from a modern incunable—the first Internet jargon lexicon. As such, it did the rounds among techies at universities like MIT and Stanford during the days of the Internet's early development. This lexicon was an open-source offering and continued to invite free use even after its elaboration and publication as a hacker's dictionary. I am surely not the only one to feel affectionately disposed—and even more operatively indebted—to its fashioners, notably Guy L. Steele and Eric S. Raymond. The originators (like the guys responsible, way back when, for RACTER's "The Policeman's Beard Is Half-Constructed") were clearly an extraordinary crew, computer geeks who were not only smart but also funny, fascinated by varieties of language, gifted with wit, and inclined to lexicographic nuance. I assembled the second poem explicitly as a tribute to some of these people, keeping in mind the degree to which all writing is a tribute to its sources in the sense-works of the world, existing networks of sensory datum we pick apart and then reorganize, by our own inner lights.

I might add that my own work had itself been expropriated in the name of art, nearly two decades before I fashioned "Hackers Can Sidejack Cookies." The British artist Tom Phillips in a book called *Where Are They Now?* used poems of mine as raw material for one of his revisions-via-partial-deletion; those deletions always leave, in their wake, new verbal networks (though I can't say it felt entirely comfortable being in the same boat with W. H. Mallock). My own way of imposing on a textual source (for my poem twenty years later) was this: I rearranged snippets by a loony lyric logic, and supplemented them, toward the poem's end, with a whiff of extravagant narrative.

That's how my version comes to feature the networker himself, caught up (ultimately) in some deeper networks than he thinks, of neural or chemical bonding, fellow-feeling, family love—some version of the live affiliations circumstantiating work's occasion all that time. What keeps us moved or moving. Out of the box. Not just unpacked, but somehow overflowing every virtual (and verbal) artifact.

—Victoria, BC, December 31, 2010

ETYMOLOGICAL DIRGE

"Twas grace that taught my heart to fear."

Calm comes from burning.
Tall comes from fast.
Comely doesn't come from come.
Person comes from mask.

The kin of charity is whore,
the root of charity is dear.
Incentive has its source in song
and winning in the sufferer.

Afford yourself what you can carry out.
A coward and a coda share a word.
We get our ugliness from fear.
We get our danger from the lord.

HACKERS CAN SIDEJACK COOKIES

A collage-homage to Guy L. Steele (Hacker's Dictionary)
and Eric S. Raymond (New Hacker's Dictionary)

A beige toaster is a maggotbox.
A bit bucket is a data sink.

Farkled is a synonym for hosed.
Flamage is a weenie problem.
A berserker wizard gets no score for treasure.
In MUDS one acknowledges
a bonk with an oif. (There is
a cosmic bonk/oif balance.)
A backdoor is a logic bomb.
A buttonhook is a hunchback.
Ooblick is play sludge.

There were published bang paths
ten hops long. Designs succumbing
to creeping featuritis
are banana problems.
("I know how to spell banana
but I don't know when to stop.")
Before you reconfigure, mount
a scratch monkey. A dogcow
makes a moof. An aliasing bug
can smash the stack.

(Who wrote these tunes, these runes you need
black art to parse? Don't think it's only
genius, flaming; humor, dry; a briefcase
of cerebral dust. A hat's a shark fin
and the tilde's dash is swung: but now
the daughter of the programmer
has got her period. It's all

about wetware at last—and wetware
lives in meatspace.)

Ellen Bryant Voigt

Same Bird: New Song

GROUNDHOG

not unlike otters which we love frolicking
floating on their backs like truant boys unwrapping lunch
same sleek brown pelt some overtones of gray and rust
though groundhogs have no swimming hole and lunch
is rooted in the ground beneath short legs small feet
like a fat man's odd diminutive loafers not

frolicking but scurrying layers of fat his coat
gleams as though wet shines chestnut sable darker
head and muzzle lower into the grass
a dark triangular face like the hog-nosed skunk another delicate
nose and not a snout doesn't it matter what they're called I like swine

which are smart and prefer to be clean using their snouts
to push their excrement to the side of the pen
but they have hairy skin not fur his fur
shimmers and ripples he never uproots the mother plant his teeth
I think are blunt squared off like a sheep's if cornered does he
cower like sheep or bite like a sow with a litter is he ever
attacked he looks to me inedible he shares his acreage

with moles voles ravenous crows someone
thought up the names his other name is botched Algonquin
but yes he burrows beneath the barn where once a farmer

dried cordwood he scuttles there at speech cough laugh
at lawnmower swollen brook high wind he lifts his head
as Gandhi did small tilt to the side or stands erect
like a prairie dog or a circus dog but dogs don't waddle like Mao
with a tiny tail he seems asexual like Gandhi like Jesus if Jesus
came back would he be vegetarian also pinko freako homo

in Vermont natives scornful of greyhounds from the city
self-appoint themselves woodchucks unkempt hairy macho
who would shoot on sight an actual fatso shy mild marmot radiant
as the hog-nosed skunk in the squirrel trap both cleaner than sheep
fur fluffy like a girl's maybe he is a she it matters
what we're called words shape the thought don't say
rodent and ruin everything

COW

end of the day daylight subsiding into the trees lights coming on
in the milking barns as somewhere out in the yard some ants
are tucking in their aphids for the night behind
hydrangea leaves or in their stanchions underground
they have been bred for it the smaller brain

serving the larger brain the cows eat so we will eat we guarantee
digestion is the only work they do heads down tails up
they won't have sex they get some grain some salt
no catamounts no wolves we give them names
we fertilize the fields we put up bales of hay

last week one breached the fence the neighbors
stopped to shoo it back a girl held out a handful of grass
calling the cow as you would a dog no dice
so what if she recoiled to see me burst from the house with an axe
I held it by the blade I tapped with the handle where the steaks come from

like the one I serve my friend a water sign who likes to lurk
in the plural solitude of Zen retreat to calm his mind but when it's done

what he needs I think is something truly free of mind
a slab of earth by way of cow by way of fire the surface charred
the juices running pink and red on the white plate

HOUND

since thought is prayer if hard and true I thought that thought
could lead me to compassion for my fellow creatures
insects not included contrary to the Buddha I swat them dead
the wasps might show a little compassion too I do include
the hound next door it moans all day all night a loud
slow lament a child can make itself sustain

to dramatize its misery this dog repeats repeats
he was the neighbors' child but now they have an actual child
he's been cast down to be a dog again chained outdoors heartsick
uncomprehending why can't he just buck up remember his roots his lot
not more special than any other
                         sad hound look up
at the fledglings' wide mouths look over here
at the cat teaching her litter how to hunt all sleek all black
they're interchangeable her many tits confirmed no favorites
no first no last
                at least with only two
both can be a kind of favorite it's better than three
I ought to know my sister and I each had one parent to herself
like Tea for Two it wasn't hard to be the boy
until there came the actual boy he was nothing like my father
what does it mean to have flown from the same nest into the world
you're thinking one is best
                         one open mouth no first no last but isn't it
then the parents who compete no wonder the father of animals
wanders off the best is two all right one parent and one child
we've seen it work among the elephants

FOX

rangy loping swiveling left then right I'm thinking
nonchalant but the doves flutter up to the roof of the barn the crickets
leap from the grass like fleas a fox is in my yard-o my yard-o
plenty of songs in my head

to sing to my child's child if she were here
she wakes in her wooden crib and sings to herself
odd happy child so like another child content in her pen
with a pot a metal straw a lid a hole in the lid a glass hat
for the hole a metal basket with smaller holes
one hole the size of the straw for hours

I made the pieces fit then took them apart
then made them fit when I got tired I lay me down my little head
against the flannel chicks and ducks then slept then woke then took
the puzzle up my mother had another child sick unto death
she needed me to fall in love with solitude I fell in love
it is my toy my happiness the child of my friends
is never ever left alone asleep awake
pushing her wooden blocks around the rug they cannot bear
her least distress their eyes stay on their sparrow poor happy child

last year I startled a fox crossing the road the tail
more rust than red the head cranked forward facing me
it stopped stock-still as if deciding whether to hurry forward
or turn back it had a yellow apple in its mouth
and the little ones chew on the bones-o

I know I'm not alone in wanting, after every completed book, some new sound,
some profoundly essential way not to repeat myself: only by changing the habit-
ual, recognizable music can one avoid what's unchallenged and self-protective.
And I'm probably not alone in having found this effort hardest, slowest, most
resistant, after putting together a volume of new and selected poems, which
looms over one's writing desk like a stone.

Luckily, my parallel project for the past decade had been a study of syntax, the poet's other (and perhaps less self-evident) rhythmic system. How that study first came into my own poems, in *Shadow of Heaven* and *Messenger: New & Selected Poems 1976–2006*, was through more complex and sustained sentence structures, often subdivided by a short fixed line that stood in sometimes violent counterpoint. When I finally began writing new poems again in 2009, I found myself at work within another option: the line was using its powers of juxtaposition not to isolate short chunks of syntax but to combine longer ones, trusting the brain to recognize the English sentence without the reinforcing "markers" of punctuation or even the surrogate punctuation of the end of the line. It sounded like both me and not me, the "self-forgetfulness" we long for.

"Groundhog" was the first of these pieces. What intrigued me, even in rough early drafts, was how speed in the line itself, combined with propulsive enjambment, could enable rapid shifts of diction and tone without endangering overall structure or clarity. These shifts seemed a good thing for a willful craftsperson, deflecting obsession away from composition and into utterance. It also required a different approach to revision—a lighter touch, a greater tolerance for repetition, a less immediate reliance on surgery and compression.

What does not interest me so much is syntactical ambiguity—I want readers to register, with some confidence, where each sentence ends; I just don't want them to rest there. But *where* to rest—and how to signal that rest without commas and colons, dashes and periods and unvarying end-stopped lines? Discovering this, poem by poem, requires a specific kind of patience, a tether for all that is headlong. But that's the key verb: to discover: why else write another line?

Acknowledgments

"Fallen" from *Intervale: New and Selected Poems* © 2001 by Betty Adcock. Reprinted with permission of Louisiana State University Press.

"Penumbra" from *Slantwise* © 2008 by Betty Adcock. Reprinted with permission of Louisiana State University Press.

"Colloquy," © 2012 by Betty Adcock. By permission of the author.

"Canter" and "Clearing the Room" from *Happily* © 2012 by Joan Aleshire. Reprinted with permission of Four Way Books. All rights reserved.

"After Vermeer" and "How to Explain Pictures to a Dead Hare" from *Fimbul-Winter* © 2010 by Debra Allbery. Reprinted with permission of Four Way Books. All rights reserved.

"Heart Valve" by Elizabeth Arnold first appeared in *Poetry* 196, no. 4 (July–August 2010). By permission of the author.

"Looking at Maps" by Elizabeth Arnold first appeared in the *Nation* (June 2011). By permission of the author.

"Daddy" and "Civilization" from *Civilization* by Elizabeth Arnold. Copyright © 2006 by Elizabeth Arnold. Used by permission of Flood Editions.

"The Spring Ephemerals" from *Midwest Eclogue* by David Baker. Copyright © 2005 by David Baker. Used by permission of W. W. Norton & Company, Inc.

"When Dean Young Talks about Wine" from *What Narcissism Means to Me* © 2003 by Tony Hoagland. Reprinted with the permission of Graywolf Press, Minneapolis, Minnesota, www.graywolfpress.org.

"Summer Sniper" (published as "Summer") from *Unincorporated Persons in the Late Honda Dynasty* @ 2010 by Tony Hoagland. Reprinted with the permission of Graywolf Press, Minneapolis, Minnesota, www.graywolfpress.org.

"Soften the Blow, Imagined God, and Give," "I Can't Do More Than This, I Can't Do Less—," "What Will We Give Up in the After Life," and "*In via est cisterna*" from *Unholy Sonnets* (Story Line Press). Copyright © 2000 by Mark Jarman. By permission of the author.

"*Metropolis,* restored edition" and "Un Chien Andalou" from *The Cineaste: Poems* by A. Van Jordan. Copyright © 2013 by A. Van Jordan. Used by permission of W. W. Norton & Company, Inc.

"O, elegant giant," "Memory of Grief," "Riddle," and "Space, in Chains," © 2012 by Laura Kasischke. By permission of the author.

"Girls' Names" from *Red Signature* by Mary Leader. Copyright © 1997 by Mary Leader. Reprinted with the permission of The Permissions Company, Inc. on behalf of Graywolf Press, Minneapolis, Minnesota, www.graywolfpress.org.

"Flamestitch Throw" by Mary Leader first appeared in *Forklift, Ohio,* no. 14 (Summer 2005). By permission of the author.

"Refuge Field," "The Mentor," and "Augur" from *Sky Burial* by Dana Levin. Copyright © 2011 by Dana Levin. Reprinted with the permission of The Permission Company, Inc. on behalf of Copper Canyon Press, www.coppercanyonpress.org.

"No Elegies" by Dana Levin first appeared in *Diode* 5, no. 2 (Winter 2012). By permission of the author.

"The Iron Key," "Mercer Street," "Night Fantasies," and "Snow" from *The Iron Key: Poems* by James Longenbach. Copyright © by James Longenbach. Used by permission of W. W. Norton & Company, Inc.

"The Pier Aspiring" and "The Shooting Zoo," from *God Particles* by Thomas Lux. Copyright © 2008 by Thomas Lux. Reprinted by permission of Houghton Mifflin Harcourt Publishing Company. All rights reserved.

"The Back Woods Ruckus," "The Persimmon Tree," "The Tin Roof the Birdsong and the Rain," "The Last Pone Gone, A Swaller in the Kettle," and "The Word Foller and Others Like It" from *The Gone and the Going Away* by Maurice Manning. Copyright © 2013 by Maurice Manning. Reprinted by permission of Houghton Mifflin Harcourt Publishing Company. All rights reserved.

"Etymological Dirge" from *The Father of the Predicaments* © 2001 by Heather McHugh and reprinted by permission of Wesleyan University Press.

"Hackers Can Sidejack Cookies" from *Upgraded to Serious*. Copyright © 2009 by Heather McHugh. Reprinted with the permission of The Permissions Company, Inc. on behalf of Copper Canyon Press, www.coppercanyonpress.org.

"The Small Canal Between Them," "It Fell on Me," "Come to Me, His Blood," "Thrombosis," and "The Concussion" from *The Beds* © 2012 by Martha Rhodes. Reprinted with permission of Autumn House Press. All rights reserved.

"Gas Station Rest Room," "Supermarket," and "Car Dealership at 3 AM" from *Night of the Republic: Poems* by Alan Shapiro. Copyright © by Alan Shapiro. Reprinted by permission of Houghton Mifflin Harcourt Publishing Company. All rights reserved.

"The Jetty" by Daniel Tobin first appeared in the *Virginia Quarterly Review* (Fall 2006); "That Is To Say," first appeared in *Christianity and Literature* (Fall 2009); "Late Bloomer" first appeared in *Image 72* (Winter 2011–12). All by permission of the author.

"Groundhog," "Cow," "Hound," and "Fox" from *Headwaters: Poems* by Ellen Bryant Voigt. Copyright © 2013 by Elen Bryant Voigt. Used by permission of W. W. Norton & Company, Inc.

"Recitation for the Dismantling of a Hydrogen Bomb" from *The Pattern More Complicated: New and Selected Poems* by Alan Williamson. Copyright © 2004 by Alan Williamson. Reprinted by permission of The University of Chicago Press.

"Event Horizon" by Alan Williamson first appeared in *Agni* 68 (Fall 2008). By permission of the author.

"Ode to Innocence" from *Reversing the Spell: New & Selected Poems*. Copyright © 1998 by Eleanor Wilner. "The Girl with Bees in Her Hair" from *The Girl with Bees in Her Hair*. Copyright © 2004 by Eleanor Rand Wilner. Both reprinted with permission of The Permissions Company, Inc. on behalf of Copper Canyon Press, www.coppercanyonpress.org.

"Influence" from *Second Person* © 2007 by C. Dale Young. Reprinted with permission of Four Way Books. All rights reserved.

"Torn" from *Torn* © 2011 by C. Dale Young. Reprinted with permission of Four Way Books. All rights reserved.

"Complaint of the Medical Illustrator" from *The Day Underneath the Day* © 2001 by C. Dale Young. Reprinted with permission of Northwestern University Press.

"The Hanged Man" by C. Dale Young first appeared in *The Collagist* (online) (April 2010). By permission of the author.

Contributors

Betty Adcock is author of six collections from Louisiana State University Press, including *Intervale: New and Selected Poems* (2001) and *Slantwise* (2008). Her work appears in many anthologies, including three Pushcart Prize volumes. Her honors include the Poets' Prize, the Texas Institute of Letters Prize, the North Carolina Governor's Medal for Literature, the Hanes Prize from the Fellowship of Southern Writers, and a Guggenheim fellowship in poetry. She is a native Texan who has spent all her writing life in North Carolina.

Joan Aleshire graduated from Radcliffe/Harvard in 1960 and received her MFA in writing from Goddard College in 1980. Her first book of poems, *Cloud Train*, was published in the AWP Awards Series in 1982; her fifth book, *Happily*, appeared from Four Way Books in April 2012. She has published poems, essays, and translations in various journals and anthologies. She has taught in the MFA Program for Writers at Warren Wilson College since 1983 and lives in Vermont.

Debra Allbery's most recent collection, *Fimbul-Winter* (Four Way, 2010), won the Grub Street National Prize in Poetry. Her previous collection, *Walking Distance*, won the Agnes Lynch Starrett Prize and was published by University of Pittsburgh Press. Other awards include two National Endowment for the Arts fellowships, the "Discovery"/*The Nation* prize, a Hawthornden fellowship, and two individual fellowships from the New Hampshire State Council on the Arts. She lives near Asheville, North Carolina, and serves as the director of the MFA Program for Writers at Warren Wilson College.

Winner of an Amy Lowell traveling grant, a Whiting Writer's award, and fellowships from the Radcliffe Institute for Advanced Study at Harvard, the

Rockefeller Foundation, and the Fine Arts Work Center, **Elizabeth Arnold** has published three books of poetry, *The Reef* (Chicago, 1999), *Civilization* (2006), and *Effacement* (Flood Editions, 2010). Her poems have appeared or are forthcoming in the *Paris Review, Poetry, Slate,* the *Kenyon Review, Conjunctions,* and the *Nation.* As a PhD student, she discovered an unpublished novel by the British poet Mina Loy, which was published by Black Sparrow Press in 1990. She teaches on the MFA faculty of the University of Maryland.

David Baker is author of ten books of poetry, most recently *Never-Ending Birds* (Norton), which won the Theodore Roethke Memorial Poetry Prize in 2011. His four prose books include *Talk Poetry: Poems and Interviews with Nine American Poets* (Arkansas, 2012) and, with Ann Townsend, *Radiant Lyre: Essays on Lyric Poetry* (Graywolf, 2007). Among his awards are prizes and grants from the Guggenheim Foundation, the National Endowment for the Arts, the Poetry Society of America, and the Society of Midland Authors. He holds the Thomas B. Fordham Chair at Denison University, in Granville, Ohio, and is poetry editor of the *Kenyon Review.*

Rick Barot has published two books of poems with Sarabande Books: *The Darker Fall* (2002) and *Want* (2008), which was a finalist for a Lambda Literary Award and received the 2009 Grub Street Book Prize. He has received fellowships and residencies from Stanford University, the National Endowment for the Arts, the Artist Trust of Washington, and Civitella Ranieri. His poems and essays have appeared in numerous publications, including *Poetry,* the *New Republic,* the *Paris Review,* the *American Poetry Review,* and the *Virginia Quarterly Review.* He lives in Tacoma, Washington, and teaches at Pacific Lutheran University.

Marianne Boruch's recent poetry collections are *The Book of Hours* (Copper Canyon, 2011) and *Grace, Fallen from* (Wesleyan, 2008); her eighth—*Cadaver, Speak*—is forthcoming (2014) from Copper Canyon. She's published two books of essays on poetry, *In the Blue Pharmacy* (Trinity, 2005) and *Poetry's Old Air* (Michigan, 1995, 2009), and a memoir, *The Glimpse Traveler* (Indiana, 2011). Her awards include the Kingsley Tufts Poetry Award; Guggenheim, National Endowment for the Arts, and Fulbright fellowships. She teaches at Purdue University, where she established the graduate creative writing program some two decades ago, and has been on faculty in the low-residency MFA Program for Writers at Warren Wilson College since 1988.

Karen Brennan is the author of six books of various genres, including the forthcoming *little dark* (Four Way, 2014) and the memoir *Being with Rachel* (Norton, 2002). She is a recipient of a National Endowment for the Arts fellowship and an Associated Writing Programs award in fiction, and her work has appeared in anthologies from Graywolf, Norton, Penguin, the University of Georgia Press, the University of Michigan Press, Longman, and Spuyten Duyvil. An emerita professor of English at the University of Utah, she has been on the faculty at the MFA Program for Writers at Warren Wilson College since 1992. The poems included in this anthology are from *The Real Enough World* (Wesleyan, 2002).

Gabrielle Calvocoressi is a temporary Texan who spends most of her time in Los Angeles. Her second book, *Apocalyptic Swing* (Persea, 2009) was a finalist for the *Los Angeles Times* Book Award. She has received fellowships from Stanford University, Civitella de Ranieri, and the Lannan Foundation. She is the poetry editor for the *Los Angeles Review of Books*.

Michael Collier's *The Ledge* (Houghton Mifflin, 2000) was a finalist for the National Book Critics Circle Award and the Los Angeles Times Book Prize. His most recent collection, *An Individual History*, appeared from Norton in 2012. He has received Guggenheim and National Endowment for the Arts fellowships, a "Discovery"/*The Nation* Award, the Alice Fay di Castagnola Award from the Poetry Society of America, and an Academy Award in Literature from the American Academy of Arts and Letters. Poet laureate of Maryland from 2001 to 2004, he teaches at the University of Maryland and is the director of the Bread Loaf Writers' Conference.

Carl Dennis has published eleven books of poetry, most recently *Callings* (Penguin, 2010). A recipient of the Pulitzer Prize and the Ruth Lilly Prize, he lives in Buffalo, New York.

Stuart Dischell is the author of *Good Hope Road*, a National Poetry Series Selection (Viking, 1993); *Evenings & Avenues* (Penguin, 1996); *Dig Safe* (Penguin, 2003); *Backwards Days* (Penguin, 2007); and the chapbooks *Animate Earth* (Jeanne Duval Editions, 1988) and *Touch Monkey* (Forklift, 2012). Dischell's poems have been published in the *Atlantic*, *Agni*, the *New Republic*, *Slate*, the *Kenyon Review*, and anthologies including *Essential Poems*, *Hammer and Blaze*, *Pushcart Prize*, and *Good Poems*. A recipient of awards from the National Endowment for the Arts, the North Carolina Arts Council, and the John Simon

Guggenheim Foundation, he teaches in the MFA Program in Creative Writing at the University of North Carolina, Greensboro.

Roger Fanning is the author of five books of poems: *The Island Itself* (A National Poetry Series Selection, 1991), *Homesick* (Penguin, 2002), *The Middle Ages* (Penguin, 2012), *The Caledonian Boar Hunt*, and *Seize the Carp: 151 Reasons Not to Kill Yourself*, a book of fragments (the last two are forthcoming). He lives in Seattle with his wife and son.

Chris Forhan is the author of three books of poetry: *Black Leapt In*, winner of the Barrow Street Press Poetry Prize (2009); *The Actual Moon, the Actual Stars* (Northwestern, 2003), winner of the Morse Poetry Prize and a Washington State Book Award; and *Forgive Us Our Happiness* (Middlebury, 1999), winner of the Bakeless Prize. He has won a National Endowment for the Arts Fellowship and two Pushcart Prizes. He lives with his wife, the poet Alessandra Lynch, and their two sons, Milo and Oliver, in Indianapolis, where he teaches at Butler University.

Reginald Gibbons has published nine books of poems, including *Creatures of a Day* (LSU, 2008, a National Book Award finalist) and *Slow Trains Overhead: Chicago Poems and Stories* (Chicago, 2010); translations of Sophocles' *Selected Poems: Odes and Fragments* (Princeton, 2008); translations of *Bacchae* (Oxford, 2009) and *Antigone* (Oxford, 2007, with the late Charles Segal); and a novel, *Sweetbitter* (LSU, 2003). He has received the Folger Shakespeare Library's O. B. Hardison Jr. Prize, the Anisfield-Wolf Book Award, and fellowships from the Guggenheim Foundation and the Center for Hellenic Studies. He is the Frances Hooper Professor of Arts and Humanities at Northwestern University and on the faculty of the MFA Program for Writers at Warren Wilson College.

Linda Gregerson's fifth collection of poetry, *The Selvage*, was published in 2012 by Houghton Mifflin Harcourt. Her many honors include awards and fellowships from the American Academy of Arts and Letters, the Kingsley Tufts Poetry Awards, the Poetry Society of America, the Guggenheim Foundation, the Rockefeller Foundation, the National Endowment for the Arts, and the Institute for Advanced Study. Gregerson is also the author of two critical books and editor, with Susan Juster, of *Empires of God: Religious Encounters in the Early Modern Atlantic World* (Pennsylvania, 2010). She teaches at the University of Michigan.

Jennifer Grotz is the author of two books of poems, *Cusp* (Houghton Mifflin/ Mariner, 2003) and *The Needle* (Houghton Mifflin Harcourt, 2011), as well as a book of translations from the French of the psalms of Patrice de La Tour du Pin. She teaches at the University of Rochester and serves as the assistant director of the Bread Loaf Writers' Conference.

Brooks Haxton's books of original poetry include six collections of shorter poems from Knopf and two book-length narrative poems. His three books of translations have been published by Viking Penguin. He has received awards and fellowships from the National Endowment for the Arts, the National Endowment for the Humanities, and the Guggenheim Foundation, among others. He has taught for twenty years at the MFA Program for Writers at Warren Wilson College and in the creative writing program at Syracuse University.

Tony Hoagland's four books of poems include *What Narcissism Means to Me* (2003) and *Donkey Gospel* (1998), both from Graywolf Press. His book of essays on poetic craft is called *Real Sofistikashun* (Graywolf, 2006). His awards include the Jackson Poetry Prize, the O. B. Hardison Jr. Prize, and the James Laughlin Award. He teaches in the creative writing program at the University of Houston and, of course, in the entymoscopic superconductor MFA Program for Writers at Warren Wilson College.

Mark Jarman's most recent collection of poetry is *Bone Fires: New and Selected Poems* (Sarabande, 2011). He has also published two books of essays about poetry, *The Secret of Poetry* (Story Line, 2001) and *Body and Soul: Essays on Poetry* (Michigan, 2002). His honors include the Lenore Marshall Prize, the Poets' Prize, and a Guggenheim fellowship in poetry. He is Centennial Professor of English, Vanderbilt University.

A. Van Jordan is the author of four collections: *Rise* (Tia Chucha, 2001), *M-A-C-N-O-L-I-A* (Norton, 2004), *Quantum Lyrics* (Norton, 2007), and *The Cineaste* (Norton, 2013). Jordan is a recipient of a Whiting Writers Award, a John Simon Guggenheim Fellowship, and a United States Artists Williams Fellowship. He is a professor in the Department of English at the University of Michigan, and he serves on the faculty of the MFA Program for Writers at Warren Wilson College.

Laura Kasischke has published eight collections of poetry and eight novels. For her most recent collection, *Space, In Chains* (Copper Canyon), she received the National Book Critics Circle Award in 2012. Her novels include *The Life before Her Eyes* (Harvest, 2002) and *In a Perfect World* (Harper, 2009). She has been the recipient of a Guggenheim fellowship and two grants from the National Endowment for the Arts. She teaches in the MFA program at the University of Michigan and lives with her husband and son in Chelsea, Michigan.

Mary Leader, while practicing law in her home state of Oklahoma, obtained her MFA from the MFA Program for Writers at Warren Wilson in 1991. Thereafter, she earned a PhD in literature from Brandeis University and has published three books of poems: *Red Signature* (Graywolf, 1997), *The Penultimate Suitor* (Iowa, 2001), and *Beyond the Fire* (Shearsman, 2010). She teaches at Purdue University, as well as at Warren Wilson.

Dana Levin's books are *In the Surgical Theatre* (1999), *Wedding Day* (2005), and *Sky Burial* (2011), all from Copper Canyon Press. A recipient of honors from the Rona Jaffe, Whiting, and Guggenheim foundations, Levin cochairs the Creative Writing and Literature Department at Santa Fe University of Art and Design in Santa Fe, New Mexico.

James Longenbach is the author of four collections of poems, most recently *The Iron Key* (Norton, 2010), as well as six books of literary criticism, most recently *The Virtues of Poetry* (Graywolf, 2013). His poems and reviews appear regularly in the *New Yorker*, the *Nation*, and the *New York Times Book Review*. A frequent faculty member at the Bread Loaf Writers' Conference and the MFA Program for Writers at Warren Wilson College, he is the Joseph Gilmore Professor of English at the University of Rochester.

Thomas Lux is Bourne Professor of Poetry at the Georgia Institute of Technology. His two most recent books are *Child Made of Sand* (poetry, Houghton Mifflin Harcourt, 2012) and *From the Southland* (nonfiction, Marick, 2012).

Maurice Manning's most recent book is *The Gone and the Going Away* (Houghton Mifflin Harcourt, 2013). His previous book, *The Common Man*, was a finalist for the Pulitzer Prize in 2010. Other books include *Bucolics* (Houghton Mifflin Harcourt, 2007), *A Companion for Owls* (Houghton Mifflin Harcourt, 2004), and *Lawrence Booth's Book of Visions* (Houghton Mifflin Harcourt, 2001), which was selected for the Yale Series of Younger Poets. He has been a fellow at the Fine Arts Work Center in Provincetown and has held a Guggenheim fellowship. Manning teaches at Transylvania University, the MFA Program for Writers at Warren Wilson, and lives in Kentucky.

Heather McHugh has taught poetry for forty years (most faithfully at the University of Washington in Seattle and at the MFA Program for Writers at Warren Wilson College in Asheville, North Carolina). She's also founder and director of CAREGIFTED (http://caregifted.org), an organization providing weeklong getaways to long-term family caregivers of the severely disabled. Her books include *Hinge & Sign: Poems, 1968–1993* (Wesleyan, 1994) and *Upgraded to Serious* (Copper Canyon, 2012).

Martha Rhodes is the author of four collections of poetry: *The Beds* (Autumn House, 2012), *Mother Quiet* (Nebraska, 2004), *Perfect Disappearance* (winner of the Green Rose Prize, New Issues, 2000), and *At the Gate* (Provincetown Arts, 1995). She teaches at Sarah Lawrence College and at the MFA Program for Writers at Warren Wilson College. She is the director of the Frost Place Festival and Conference on Poetry and a founding editor and the director of Four Way Books in New York City.

Alan Shapiro has published eleven books of poetry, most recently *Night of the Republic* (Houghton Mifflin Harcourt, 2012). A member of the American Academy of Arts and Sciences and a recipient of a Guggenheim fellowship, the Kingsley Tufts Award for *The Dead Alive and Busy* (Chicago, 2000), and a *Los Angeles Times* book award for *Mixed Company* (Chicago, 1996), he teaches at the University of North Carolina at Chapel Hill.

Daniel Tobin is the author of six books of poems, *Where the World Is Made* (New England, 1999), *Double Life* (Louisiana State, 2004); *The Narrows* (2005), *Second Things* (2008), *Belated Heavens* (2010, winner of the Massachusetts Book Award in Poetry) and *The Net* (forthcoming in 2014), all from Four Way, along with the critical studies *Passage to the Center* (Kentucky, 1999), and *Awake in America* (Notre Dame, 2007). He is the editor of *The Book of Irish American Poetry from the Eighteenth Century to the Present, Selected Early Poems of Lola Ridge* (Quale, 2007), and *Poet's Work, Poet's Play* (Michigan, 2007). His awards include fellowships from the National Endowment for the Arts and the John Simon Guggenheim Foundation.

Ellen Bryant Voigt has published seven volumes of poetry, including a new collection, *Headwaters* (2013); *Kyrie* (1996), a National Book Critics Circle Award finalist; *Shadow of Heaven* (2002), a National Book Award finalist; and *Messenger: New and Selected Poems 1976–2006*, winner of the Poets' Prize and a finalist for both the National Book Award and the Pulitzer (all are from Norton). Her essays on craft appear as *The Flexible Lyric* (Georgia, 1999) and *The Art of Syntax* (Graywolf, 2009). She has received the O. B. Hardison Jr. Prize from the Folger Shakespeare Library and a fellowship from the Academy of American Poets, where she was subsequently elected a chancellor.

Alan Williamson is a professor of English at the University of California at Davis. He has also taught at Harvard, the University of Virginia, and Brandeis. His books of poems are *Presence* (Knopf, 1983), *The Muse of Distance* (Knopf, 1988), *Love and the Soul* (1995), *Res Publica* (1998), and *The Pattern More Complicated: New and Selected Poems* (2004), all from Chicago. He has also published five critical books: *Introspection and Contemporary Poetry* (Harvard, 1984), *Pity the Monsters: The Political Vision of Robert Lowell* (New Haven, 1974), *Eloquence and Mere Life* (Michigan, 1994), *Almost a Girl: Male Writers and Female Identification* (Virginia, 2001), and *Westernness: A Meditation* (Virginia, 2006). He has received grants from the National Endowment for the Arts and the Guggenheim Foundation.

Eleanor Wilner is the author of seven books of poems, most recently *Tourist in Hell* (Chicago, 2010), *The Girl with Bees in Her Hair* (2004), and *Reversing the Spell: New and Selected Poems* (1998) (Copper Canyon); a verse translation of Euripides' *Medea* (Pennsylvania, 1998); and a book on visionary imagination. Her awards include a MacArthur Foundation Fellowship, the Juniper Prize, Pushcart Prizes, and a National Endowment for the Arts grant. A forty-year veteran of teaching, she has taught for over twenty years for the MFA Program for Writers at Warren Wilson College.

C. Dale Young is the author of three collections of poetry: *The Day Underneath the Day* (Northwestern, 2001); *The Second Person* (Four Way, 2007) and *Torn* (Four Way, 2011). He practices medicine full-time, edits poetry for the *New England Review*, and teaches in the MFA Program for Writers at Warren Wilson College. A recipient of various grants and awards, he is a 2012 Poetry Fellow of the John Simon Guggenheim Memorial Foundation. He lives in San Francisco.